Curt's jolie —
This book is for
my best friends Mon
happy recipes for you
with love,
the McLachlin
:)

# DIG IN!

## A Collection of Family Favorites

Judy Chemers

ISBN 978-1-312-47239-6

Lulu Publishing; www.lulu.com

# Gathering around the table...

to share tastes and life is what food is all about. I find great joy in the gesture of offering something delicious to the people I love. We're a family who likes to cook and loves to eat. Every family has their favorite dishes and mine is no different. This book includes the favorites of my husband and daughters, as well as favorites of my mom, sisters and brother.

I've been collecting cookbooks and recipes for years. The recipes included here are either my own creation or were inspired by other recipes. Like many home cooks, I follow the recipe the first time and subsequently make changes to suit my family's tastes.

When my daughters first suggested that I work on a cookbook of their favorites, I could only think of a handful of recipes they would want to include. It was only a short week later that I received a lengthy list, thus beginning a journey that has been a true labor of love. That journey has culminated with a book that offers over 200 recipes, many of which I hope, now that they are married and having children, will become their family's favorites as well.

You can always spot someone's favorite cookbook by its pages; a pristinely clean book has not been used, much less loved. Oh, the joy of pages that have been spilled upon, for they are the tried and true favorites. I delight in imagining that someday this book will have a number of soiled pages that represent your family's favorites.

I raise my glass to you and offer "Cheers" to your gatherings, large and small, filled with laughter, love and good food!

## Dedicated with Love and Happy Bellies

To my longtime biggest fan, critic and 'taste' bud, my husband, Barry.

To my extraordinary daughters, Laura and Julia, who are delightfully adventurous cooks and who mean the world to me. Here you go, girls...
Dig in!

# DIG IN TO...

~

*A list of recipes may be found on each chapter page.*

# Details...

You'll notice my recipes do not have serving sizes indicated; I've found that they can be misleading. However, you'll be able to get an idea of how many may be served by seeing how many chicken breasts or how much pasta, etc., is in a recipe. My family has pretty healthy appetites (read as big portions!), but I know not everyone does.

Even when using the same recipe, we usually get different results. The freshness of ingredients and usage of different brands contribute to this. It's true - buy the best quality and freshest ingredients you can and your results will be better. There are so many other little things that factor into this that I decided to list, in no particular order, some of the nuances of my cooking habits and little tips that may make cooking and baking a bit easier.

*Cooking and Baking:*
• Read the recipe in its entirety before beginning.
• Slice and chop vegetables uniformly so they cook evenly.
• Go easy on salt when using salty cheese, such as Parmesan or Feta.
• When measuring Parmesan, place the measuring cup on wax paper. Grate into the cup, and when the measure is full, rap it on the counter a couple of times to settle the cheese and then grate more to fill it. Rap and fill again until measure is full. A rotary grater works well for grating.
• When cooking pasta, season the water generously with salt when it begins to boil.
• When cooking pasta, dip a measuring cup or coffee mug in the water right before draining; the pasta water can aid in creating a sauce or thinning one.
• Crush dried herbs, like oregano and basil, in your palms before adding.
• When seasoning with pepper, salt or dried herbs, hold the pepper mill or sprinkle the salt or herb about 12" or so above the item being seasoned. This will allow the seasoning to be distributed more evenly.

• For finely grated citrus zest, use very short strokes on a microplane. Zest the colored part only; the white pith is bitter.

• When making vinaigrettes, first combine all of the ingredients, except the oil; this helps the salt and sugar dissolve better. Add the oil when the other ingredients are well blended.

• Shrimp are measured by how many are in a pound. The designation U-10 or U-15, etc. means there are under 10 or under 15 shrimp in a pound; thus, the lower the number, the larger the shrimp.

• When putting both wet and dry ingredients into the food processor work bowl, put wet in first. The dry will be less likely to stick to the bottom or corners.

• Sprinkling watery produce, such as zucchini, tomatoes or watermelon, with a little kosher salt and allowing them to stand for a period of time draws the water out and intensifies their natural flavor.

• Orange and grapefruit supremes are membrane-free segments of fruit. To cut citrus supremes, trim the top and bottom of the fruit. Set it on one cut end and carefully cut away the peel and pith, following the curve of the fruit. Holding the fruit, slide the knife into the fruit on either side of the segment's membrane; release supreme. If using the juice in the recipe, hold the fruit over a bowl to catch the juice. If more juice is needed, squeeze the membrane core into the bowl.

• A garlic press is easier to clean when the cloves are not peeled.

• When measuring honey, corn syrup or maple syrup, first spray the measure with cooking spray so the item slides out easily.

• To toast nuts, spread them on a rimmed baking sheet. Bake at 350° for about 6 - 10 minutes. Nuts burn quickly, so be sure to keep a close eye on them.

• After trying several brands of kosher salt, I prefer Morton's.

• When brushing butter on phyllo, use a new 2"-wide paintbrush with soft, black bristles. You'll get better coverage than with a pastry brush and if a bristle falls out you'll be able to spot it right away.

• When freezing items in a zip-top bag, use a freezer bag and squeeze out as much air as possible. The dry freezer air causes the item to dry out.

• When pasta is cooked in a recipe and reheated as leftovers, it may get mushy. There are a couple of ways to avoid this: 1) If you're making more than what you need that day, like a big pot of soup, transfer what you won't need to a storage container before adding the uncooked pasta to the pot. When heating the stored portion, add the uncooked pasta once the portion is hot. 2) Cook and store the pasta separately, adding to each serving rather than the whole pot.

• When using the food processor to mince garlic and chop vegetables, mince the garlic before chopping the vegetables; garlic minces better in a dry work bowl. Drop the peeled cloves through the feed tube while the machine is running, then transfer the garlic onto a piece of wax paper, fold it over and set it aside until needed; proceed with chopping the vegetables.

• To avoid sliced onions having a semi-circle shape, slice them by cutting in half through the ends, trimming the ends and slicing each half vertically.

• Clean mushrooms by wiping them with a damp paper towel rather than holding them under a running faucet.

• Peel mango by lightly scoring skin vertically in quarters, then peel each quarter.

• If you don't prefer the sharp taste of raw onions, such as when they're served in a salad, soak them in water for about 10 minutes to help mellow them a bit.

• When refrigerating a cooked and cooled item that is stored in a container with a lid, place a paper towel under the lid (it may stick out a bit) to collect any condensation. After the item is thoroughly chilled, discard the towel.

• Fluff cooked rice with a fork rather than a spoon, as a spoon tends to mash the grains.

• When refrigerating or freezing something in a zip-top bag or covering it with plastic wrap before baking, use a Sharpie to write the final baking instructions on the plastic.


*Baking only:*
• Replace baking powder annually.

• Buy an extra set of dry measuring cups and keep the ½-cup in the sugar container and the 1-cup in the flour container.

• To measure flour, keep a chopstick in the container, trimming it, if necessary, to fit. Stir the flour with the chopstick to aerate, scoop it into the measuring cup and level it off with the chopstick.

• When using a stand mixer and instructed to "combine dry ingredients" in a recipe, place the dry ingredients in the mixer bowl before beginning. Mix at low speed for about 1 minute and transfer the dry ingredients to a sheet of aluminum foil or a bowl, setting aside until needed.

• When a cake is in the oven, do not slam doors or cabinets, or the cake may fall.

• Separate eggs when cold.

• Beat egg whites at room temperature.

• For best results with whipped cream, chill the bowl and beaters prior to whipping.

• For even baking in most ovens, rotate the pan halfway through the baking time. If using two racks for pans, rotate pans and switch racks halfway through the baking time.

• When baking cookies, use a cookie sheet with only one side up so the cookies can carefully slide right off the sheet onto a wire rack for cooling.

• When greasing the pan, take a smidge of the beaten or melted butter and smear it using either the wrap from the butter or a small piece of wax paper.

• When using a stand mixer, be sure to stop the machine from time to time and scrape down the sides and bottom of the bowl to ensure the thorough blending of ingredients.

• Have several wire racks on hand for cooling. Since the rack the pan is cooled on becomes hot, do not use that same rack to cool a cake or cookies when they're removed from the pan.

• When baking a two-layer cake and wanting the same amount of batter in each pan so the layers bake evenly, stand a toothpick up in one of the pans of cake batter and twirl it between your fingers. Place the same toothpick in the second pan and twirl to see if the batter is at the same level.

• When positioning the layers of a 2-layer cake, invert the top layer over the frosted bottom layer.

# Appetizers

Tropical Salsa • 14
Marinated Mushrooms • 15
Spicy Red Pepper and Eggplant Caponata • 16
Mushroom and Leek Pinwheels • 17
Skewered Tortellini and Peppers • 18
Tortilla Española • 19
Pesto Palmiers • 20
Basil Pesto • 21
Sun-Dried Tomato Pesto • 21
The Cheese Plate • 22
Cheddar Pecan Wafers • 24
Baked Brie and Apricot in Puff Pastry • 25
Stuffed Dates • 26
Ceviche • 27
Shrimp Salsa • 28
Savory Triangle Puffs • 29

~

# Tropical Salsa

*This is Laura's go-to summer salsa... and her husband, Darren, loves to go to it!*

½ fresh pineapple, cored and chopped
1 ripe mango, chopped
½ cup red onion, diced
1 red bell pepper, diced
1 jalapeno, minced
2 - 3 limes, juiced
¼ cup minced fresh cilantro leaves
½ teaspoon kosher salt
1 tablespoon canola oil
1 avocado, diced

tortilla chips

Combine all ingredients, adding avocado last, and refrigerate for several hours.

Serve with chips.


Suggestion~
This salsa also works well when served on top of grilled shrimp, fish or chicken.

# Marinated Mushrooms

4 garlic cloves, minced
6 scallions, thinly sliced
½ bunch flat-leaf parsley, leaves finely chopped
¾ cup red wine vinegar
3 tablespoons sugar
1½ teaspoons kosher salt
1 tablespoon fresh lemon juice
2 teaspoons Worcestershire
1 teaspoon freshly ground black pepper
¼ teaspoon yellow mustard
1 cup olive oil
3 pounds button mushrooms

In a large container with a lid, combine all ingredients, except oil and mushrooms; shake well. Add oil and shake well. Add mushrooms, cover and gently shake to coat mushrooms.

Refrigerate overnight, shaking container periodically. Taste and adjust seasoning.

Serve at room temperature.

# Spicy Red Pepper and Eggplant Caponata

4 large red bell peppers, large chop
1½-pound eggplant, peeled and large chop
6 garlic cloves, minced
2 15-ounce cans chopped tomatoes, drained well in a mesh strainer
3 ounces olive oil
¾ teaspoon kosher salt
½ teaspoon dried red pepper flakes
6 tablespoons balsamic vinegar, divided

Preheat oven to 400°. Combine all ingredients, except balsamic vinegar, in a large bowl. Divide the mixture between two large rimmed baking sheets and arrange vegetables in a single layer.

Roast for 1 - 1½ hours, switching racks halfway through and stirring occasionally. Cook until vegetables are very tender, taking care they do not get dry. During the last 10 minutes, stir 3 tablespoons vinegar into each pan. Remove from oven and cool.

When vegetables are cool, chop to desired size. Refrigerate for up to one week.

Serve at room temperature.


Suggestion~
Serve on lightly toasted baguette slices spread with goat cheese or place in a bowl and serve with pita chips.

This can also work as a vegetarian entrée; toss the hot caponata with a shaped pasta, such as farfalle, shell or rotini, and finish with a grating of fresh Parmesan.

# Mushroom and Leek Pinwheels

*My mushroom-loving daughter, Julia, loves these pinwheels!*

4 tablespoons unsalted butter
1½ pounds mushrooms, finely chopped
½ cup chopped leeks, white and light green part only
1 tablespoon minced garlic
¾ cup low-sodium chicken broth
12 ounces cream cheese, cut into chunks
½ teaspoon kosher salt
¼ teaspoon freshly ground black pepper
¼ cup chopped flat-leaf parsley leaves
1 package Pepperidge Farm frozen puff pastry sheets, refrigerated
    overnight

In a large skillet, melt butter over medium-high heat. Add mushrooms and sauté for 3 - 4 minutes. Stir in leeks and garlic; cook 2 minutes. Add broth and cook until liquid has evaporated.

Reduce heat to low and add cream cheese, stirring until cheese is melted. Add salt and pepper and stir in parsley. Transfer to a bowl and refrigerate until well chilled.

Place one pastry sheet on a lightly floured surface and roll out to 14" x 12". Spread half the filling to the edges, leaving a ½" border along one of the long sides. Working from the long side with the filling to the edge, roll up tightly to the border. Moisten the pastry and finish rolling, gently pressing to seal. Repeat with second pastry sheet.

Preheat oven to 450°. Cut pastry into ¼" slices using a serrated knife. Place slices on a parchment-lined cookie sheet and bake for about 12 minutes. Turn pinwheels over and bake an additional 5 - 8 minutes, or until golden brown. Serve immediately.


Suggestion~
To make ahead and freeze, wrap rolled pastry tightly in plastic, then aluminum foil and place in a freezer zip-top bag; freeze up to 3 weeks. Thaw in the refrigerator overnight before slicing and baking.

# Skewered Tortellini and Peppers

2 tablespoons tarragon vinegar
1½ teaspoons Dijon mustard
½ teaspoon dried tarragon
½ teaspoon sugar
½ teaspoon kosher salt
freshly ground black pepper, to taste
⅓ cup olive oil
9-ounce package fresh cheese tortellini
1 red pepper, room temperature and cut into ½" squares
1 orange or yellow pepper, room temperature and cut into ½" squares

6" wood skewers

Whisk vinegar, mustard, tarragon, sugar, salt and pepper in a bowl large enough to hold the tortellini and peppers. Whisk in oil; set aside.

Cook tortellini according to package directions. Add peppers to cook with the tortellini the last minute of cooking; drain very well. Immediately add tortellini and peppers to the container with vinaigrette and stir gently to combine. Gently stir tortellini and peppers periodically as they cool. When completely cool, cover and refrigerate overnight.

Hold each tortellini in a 'C' shape and run the skewer through vertically, then skewer a pepper square, taking care to keep both the tortellini and pepper close to the pointy end of the skewer. Arrange the skewers on a platter.

Bring to room temperature before serving.

The marinated tortellini will keep for several days refrigerated.

# Tortilla Española

*When we visited Laura in Madrid, she took us to several 'caves.' The caves were actually bars that featured specialty tapas along with sangria. We all loved the tortilla. Spanish tortilla is not the tortilla we're accustomed to; rather, it is more akin to a potato omelet. When she came home at the end of the semester, I made this tortilla and we toasted her return... with sangria, of course!*

¾ cup olive oil
1¼ pounds Yukon gold or red potatoes, peeled and large chop
1¼ cups chopped sweet yellow onion
1½ teaspoons kosher salt, divided
5 large eggs
freshly ground black pepper

In a 10" nonstick skillet, heat oil over medium heat. When oil is hot, add potatoes, onion and half the salt. Reduce the heat a bit and cook, stirring occasionally, until vegetables are tender, about 45 minutes. Drain them in a colander set over a bowl and cool 5 minutes.

In a large bowl, lightly beat eggs and stir in the cooked vegetables. Add the remaining salt and pepper, to taste. Add 1 tablespoon of oil from the bowl.

Heat 1 tablespoon oil from the bowl in the same skillet and add the vegetable-egg mixture, pressing the potatoes down. Cook, covered, over low heat for about 12 - 15 minutes, or until almost set. Turn off heat, keep covered and let stand 15 minutes. Shake the skillet to be sure tortilla is set on the bottom and not sticking.

Invert tortilla onto a large plate and slide it back into the skillet, bottom-side up. Cook, covered, over low heat for an additional 15 minutes, or until set.

Slide onto serving platter and cut into wedges. Serve warm or at room temperature.

# Pesto Palmiers

*These are one of Laura's absolute favorites!*

1 package Pepperidge Farm frozen puff pastry sheets, refrigerated
   overnight
⅔ cup pesto, divided
1½ cups Parmesan-Reggiano, divided
1 egg, beaten with 2 teaspoons water

~

Place one pastry sheet on a lightly floured surface and roll out to 18" x 11".

Spread ⅓ cup of pesto over the surface, then sprinkle with ¾ cup of
Parmesan. Lay a sheet of wax paper over Parmesan and gently press the
Parmesan into the dough by using a rolling pin; discard plastic.

From the long side, tightly roll pastry to the middle of the sheet, then tightly
roll the other long side to the middle of the sheet.

Cut pastry into ¼" slices using a serrated knife. Place slices, cut side down,
on a parchment-lined cookie sheet; press lightly with palm to flatten.
Refrigerate 15 minutes.

Preheat oven to 400°. Remove sheet from refrigerator and brush palmiers
with egg wash. Repeat with second pastry sheet.

Bake for 10 - 15 minutes, or until golden brown. Transfer to paper towels
and let cool. If making a few hours in advance, store loosely in aluminum
foil at room temperature.

One sheet of puff pastry makes about 36 palmiers.


Suggestion~
To make ahead and freeze, cut rolled pastry in half. Wrap each tightly in
plastic, then aluminum foil and place in a zip-top bag; freeze up to 3 weeks.
Thaw in the refrigerator overnight before slicing and baking.

# Basil Pesto

3 large garlic cloves
2 cups packed fresh basil leaves
¾ cup freshly grated Parmesan-Reggiano
¼ cup pine nuts, toasted
¼ cup olive oil
kosher salt
freshly ground black pepper

With machine running, drop garlic through the feed tube of a food
processor to mince. Place basil in work bowl and process until finely
minced. Add cheese and nuts; process. With machine running, pour oil
into the pusher and process until emulsified. Add salt and pepper, to taste.


# Sun~Dried Tomato Pesto

1 small to medium garlic clove
½ cup oil-packed sun-dried tomatoes, drained and oil reserved
½ cup chopped fresh basil leaves
¼ teaspoon sugar
¼ teaspoon kosher salt
⅛ teaspoon freshly ground black pepper

With machine running, drop garlic through the feed tube of a food
processor to mince. Add remaining ingredients to work bowl and process
until a thick paste forms. Add reserved oil, as needed, for consistency.


Suggestion~
If you typically use small amounts of pesto, place the pesto in ice cube trays
until solid. Pop out the cubes and transfer them to a freezer zip-top bag and
store in the freezer. When needed, the cubes thaw pretty quickly at room
temperature.

# The Cheese Plate

*Both of my daughters love cheese and are adept at choosing and displaying cheeses when they entertain. I asked Julia for her thoughts on cheese plates and received the following... which is wonderfully comprehensive!*

*Crowd-pleasing cheeses:*
Spreadable ~ goat, Brie, ricotta, Feta
Blue ~ Maytag, Gorgonzola, Cambozola
Soft ~ Gouda, aged Cheddar, Jarlsberg
Hard ~ Parmesan-Reggiano, Pecorino

Whether serving a small (2-3) or large (4+) cheese plate, offer cheese wedges or wheels from different categories. Remove cheese/s from the refrigerator about an hour before serving to bring to room temperature.

*Favorite accents:*
Savory ~ toasted nuts, fresh olives, Balsamic or other flavored vinegar, prosciutto, flavored olive oil
Sweet ~ toasted nuts, fresh or dried fruit, fruit jam, honey, Balsamic or other flavored vinegar

In general, envision a 'bite combo' for every cheese, choosing the accents that complement the cheese best. If offering only one cheese, consider serving both savory and sweet accents to make it feel a little more varied.

*Suggestions for seasonal combinations (beginning with Spring):*
• Triple Crème Brie, strawberries and chopped hazelnuts
• goat or ricotta mixed with honey and black pepper, fresh figs, strawberries or pitted fresh cherries
• Bocconcini (mini semi-soft mozzarella balls), cherry or grape tomatoes, Balsamic vinegar, basil or sun-dried tomato pesto (page 21)
• Feta, watermelon and/or cucumber and fresh basil
• Pecorino or Brie, seedless blackberry jam, fresh basil and walnut halves
• aged Gouda or Cheddar and thinly sliced tart apples
• Pecorino, Parmesan-Reggiano or Ricotta and rosemary-roasted grapes
• Cambozola, aged Gouda or Jarlsberg, grapes or sliced ripe pears and pecan halves
• Gorgonzola, dried apricots or dates and walnut halves
• Ricotta or Mozzarella and sun-dried tomatoes
• Parmesan-Reggiano, prosciutto and Balsamic vinegar

*Vehicle:*
Crostini ~ for spreadable cheeses and dipping in flavored oils
Thin crackers ~ one plain and one or two flavored

*Presentation:*
Serving platter ~ wooden board, ceramic platter, marble or slate slab
Knives/slicer ~ one for each cheese
Small bowls ~ for olives, nuts, honey, jam and oil
Small cruets ~ for vinegars
Leaves ~ use large, non-poisonous and pesticide-free leaves, such as grape, lemon or hydrangea

Unwrap cheese/s and place on a large platter, tucking a leaf or two under the wedge or wheel. (Do not pre-cut cheese.) Surround cheese/s with accents (nuts and dried fruit may be placed in a small bowl or mounded on the platter), taking care not to crowd the platter. If the platter has enough space, include the crostini and crackers; if not, arrange them in a napkin-lined basket.

Suggestion~
At the end of a meal, a cheese plate with sweet accents may be offered in lieu of a traditional dessert.

# Cheddar Pecan Wafers

1 cup flour
½ teaspoon kosher salt
¼ teaspoon cayenne
½ cup unsalted butter, diced and frozen for 20 minutes
2 cups grated Cheddar
½ chopped toasted pecans

Place flour, salt and cayenne in a food processor work bowl and process to blend. Add butter and cheese; process/pulse to combine. When mixture is clumpy, add pecans and pulse until incorporated. Place dough on a lightly-floured surface and press into a ball.

Lay out 2 sheets of plastic wrap. Divide dough in half and place each half on the plastic. Form into a 1½" diameter log as best you can (dough will be soft). Roll log up in the plastic and refrigerate for 1 hour.

Working with one log at a time, place unwrapped log on a work surface and roll it a bit so it is smooth and even in diameter. Roll it in a new piece of plastic wrap and refrigerate for at least 4 hours. Repeat with second log.

Preheat oven to 375°. Slice ¼" rounds and place them on a parchment-lined cookie sheet. Bake for 8 - 10 minutes. Slide parchment off sheet and let cool before serving.


Suggestion~
To make ahead and freeze, wrap each log tightly in plastic, then aluminum foil and place in a zip-top bag; freeze up to 2 months. Thaw in the refrigerator overnight before slicing and baking.

# Baked Brie and Apricot in Puff Pastry

*For a savory baked Brie option, you may want to consider 'Baked Brie with Caramelized Onions' in the Thanksgiving chapter.*

1 package Pepperidge Farm frozen puff pastry sheets, refrigerated
   overnight
1-pound wheel whole Brie
8 - 12 ounces apricot preserves
1 egg, beaten with 2 teaspoons water

sliced baguette
crackers

Preheat oven to 375°. On a lightly floured surface, lightly roll out one pastry sheet and place Brie on top. Cut out a circle 2" larger than Brie; set circle aside.

Lightly roll out the second pastry sheet and place Brie on top. Cut out a circle 1" larger than Brie and press pastry up the sides. Set on a parchment-lined rimmed baking sheet.

Spread preserves evenly over top of Brie. Brush egg wash on sides of pastry and quickly place reserved pastry circle on top of preserves, pressing sides down to seal.

Brush remaining egg wash over pastry and down sides. If desired, cut out decorative shapes from excess pastry and place on top. Brush cut-outs with egg wash.

Bake for 25 - 35 minutes. Let cool 10 minutes. Transfer to a platter and serve with sliced baguette or crackers.

# Stuffed Dates

*There are no measurements listed since you can make whatever quantity you desire. Keep in mind that for every two dates served, you'll need one slice of bacon. It doesn't get much easier or tastier than this!*

Medjool dates
Blue, Parmesan-Reggiano, Asiago, Pecorino or Manchego cheese
Applewood or Black Forest bacon, cut in half crosswise

Preheat oven to 425°. Cut a slit on the side of each date and remove the pit. Insert cheese into the cavity and pinch the slit closed. Wrap the date with half a slice of bacon and secure with a toothpick.

Place dates on an aluminum foil-lined rimmed baking sheet. Bake for 6 - 10 minutes, or until bacon is browned on the bottom. Turn dates over and bake an additional 6 - 10 minutes. Transfer the stuffed dates to a paper towel and let cool for 5 minutes. Remove toothpicks and serve.

# Ceviche

1 cup fresh orange juice
⅓ cup fresh lime juice
⅓ cup fresh lemon juice
1 mango, diced
1 jalapeno, minced
½ cup minced red onion
¼ cup minced fresh cilantro leaves + a few whole leaves for garnish
¼ teaspoon kosher salt
1 pound sea scallops, side muscle removed, if present
1 avocado, diced

Combine all ingredients, except scallops and avocado. Cut scallops into quarters and add to juice mixture.

Refrigerate at least six hours to 'cook' the scallops. Stir periodically, taking care to submerge scallops in the juice. When ready, scallops will be opaque in the center. Stir in avocado and serve chilled in small bowls garnished with cilantro.


Suggestion~
The mango may be substituted with chopped cherry or grape tomatoes.

The scallops may be cut smaller and served with tortilla chips.

# Shrimp Salsa

2 large tomatoes, seeded and diced
½ red onion, diced
½ red pepper, diced
½ yellow pepper, diced
1 cup diced jicama
½ English cucumber, peeled and diced
kernels from 1 ear white corn
2 tablespoons chopped fresh cilantro leaves
2 tablespoons chopped fresh flat-leaf parsley leaves
2 jalapenos, finely chopped
2 tablespoons fresh lime juice
½ teaspoon kosher salt
¼ teaspoon freshly ground black pepper
2 avocados, diced
½ pound cooked shrimp, chilled and diced

tortilla chips

Combine all ingredients, except avocado and shrimp, and refrigerate for several hours.

Gently stir in avocado and shrimp just before serving. Serve with chips.

# Savory Triangle Puffs

1 tablespoon olive oil
1 small sweet yellow onion, finely chopped
1 tablespoon fresh ginger, minced
1 teaspoon ground coriander
1 teaspoon chili powder
½ teaspoon kosher salt
¼ teaspoon cumin
2 small garlic cloves, minced
1 Granny Smith or other tart apple, peeled and chopped
4 chicken tenderloins, cut into small dice
½ cup low-sodium chicken broth
1 package Pepperidge Farm frozen puff pastry sheets, refrigerated
   overnight
1 egg, beaten

In a skillet, heat oil over medium heat and sauté onion, ginger and
seasonings, cooking until the onion is soft. Reduce heat and stir in garlic
and apple; cook until the apple is soft. Add chicken and cook 3 - 4 minutes,
or until
it is just cooked through. Transfer mixture to a bowl and allow it to cool
completely.

Preheat oven to 400°. On a lightly floured surface, roll out one sheet of
pastry to a 12" square. Cut into sixteen 3" squares. Place a rounded
teaspoonful of filling in the center of each square. Moisten the edges
with water and fold in half diagonally. Use fork tines to press edges
together to seal.

Brush the puffs with the egg and pierce tops with a fork. Bake on a
parchment-lined cookie sheet for 15 minutes. Let cool 5 minutes before
serving.


Suggestion~
Puffs may be assembled ahead, frozen on a cookie sheet, and then placed
in a freezer zip-top bag. Thaw in the refrigerator overnight and apply the
egg wash before baking.

# Starter and Entrée Soups

Asparagus Soup • 32
Roasted Butternut Squash Soup • 33
Carrot Soup • 34
Moroccan Carrot Soup • 35
Wild Mushroom Soup • 36
Cheesy Mushroom Onion Soup • 37
Roasted Tomato Soup • 38
Minestrone • 39
Pasta e Fagioli • 40
Italian Vegetable Soup • 41
Mushroom Barley Soup • 42
Mulligatawny • 43
Chicken Coconut Soup • 44
Chicken Soup • 45
Cheesy Chicken Chowder with Cauliflower • 46
White Corn Tortilla Soup • 47
Chilled Minted Pea Soup • 48
Gazpacho • 49

~

# Asparagus Soup

*This is a long-time favorite of our family. Unless we're having a formal dinner, I usually serve it in mugs prior to sitting down at the table.*

4 tablespoons unsalted butter
2 large sweet yellow onions, chopped
2 pounds asparagus, cut into ½" pieces, tough ends discarded
2 14-ounce cans low-sodium chicken broth
kosher salt
freshly ground black pepper

In a 4-quart saucepan, melt butter over medium-low heat and sauté onions until soft. Add asparagus and sauté another 10 minutes.

Add broth and bring to a boil. Reduce heat and let soup simmer until asparagus pieces are very soft.

Remove from heat and cool 10 minutes; purée with an immersion blender until smooth. Season to taste with salt and pepper. Reheat before serving.

# Roasted Butternut Squash Soup

6 cups 1" chunks butternut squash (about 2 pounds cut up)
kosher salt
freshly ground black pepper
4 tablespoons unsalted butter
1 sweet yellow onion, chopped
2 medium-sized Granny Smith apples, peeled and chopped
12 fresh sage leaves, torn into small pieces
5 - 6 cups low-sodium chicken broth
>1½ teaspoons kosher salt
freshly ground black pepper, to taste

Preheat oven to 425°. Line a large rimmed baking sheet with aluminum foil and spray with non-stick cooking spray. Arrange squash on foil in an even layer, season with salt and pepper, and roast for 45 - 60 minutes, depending on size of chunks.

After squash has roasted about 20 minutes, begin the soup by melting butter in a 4-quart saucepan over medium heat and sauté the onions, apples and sage leaves until onions are soft. Stir in the roasted squash, 5 cups of broth, salt and pepper. Raise heat to medium-high and bring to a boil. Reduce heat to medium-low and simmer 15 minutes.

Remove from heat and cool 10 minutes; purée with an immersion blender. Add more broth, if needed, to obtain desired consistency. Reheat before serving.

Suggestion~
Butternut squash can be a difficult vegetable to cut; picking up a package of pre-cut cubes makes this soup much easier to prepare.

# Carrot Soup

3 tablespoons unsalted butter
2 sweet yellow onions, chopped
2 pounds carrots, chopped
1 potato, peeled and chopped
1 bay leaf
3 14-ounce cans low-sodium chicken broth
½ teaspoon sugar
½ teaspoon ground ginger
kosher salt, to taste
freshly ground black pepper, to taste

In a 4-quart saucepan, melt butter over medium-low heat and sauté onions and carrots for 5 minutes. Cover pan and cook until vegetables are soft, about 10 minutes. Add remaining ingredients and simmer for 40 minutes.

Remove from heat, discard bay leaf and cool 10 minutes; purée soup with an immersion blender until smooth. Taste and adjust seasoning. Reheat before serving.

# Moroccan Carrot Soup

3 tablespoons unsalted butter
2 sweet yellow onions, chopped
2 pounds carrots, chopped
1 teaspoon ground cinnamon
½ teaspoon ground ginger
½ teaspoon kosher salt
¼ teaspoon freshly ground black pepper
pinch cayenne pepper
3 14-ounce cans low-sodium chicken broth
½ cup fresh orange juice
sugar, to taste

¼ cup chopped fresh mint

In a 4-quart saucepan, melt butter over medium heat and cook onions until tender. Add carrots and cook 5 minutes.

Stir in seasonings; cook for 2 - 3 minutes. Add broth and bring to a boil. Reduce heat and simmer until the carrots are tender.

Remove from heat and cool 10 minutes; purée with an immersion blender until smooth. Add orange juice and sugar; reheat before serving.

Serve garnished with mint.

# Wild Mushroom Soup

*This full-flavored mushroom soup is one that Laura shared and one that we love.*

4 tablespoons butter
2 cups diced sweet yellow onion
8 ounces crimini mushrooms, chopped
8 ounces fresh oyster mushrooms, chopped
8 ounces fresh shiitake mushrooms, stems removed and caps chopped
kosher salt
freshly ground black pepper
1½ tablespoons fresh thyme leaves, chopped
¼ cup dry sherry or brandy
2 tablespoons flour
2 14-ounce cans low-sodium chicken broth

¼ cup minced fresh flat-leaf parsley leaves

Melt butter in a 4-quart saucepan over medium-high heat. Add onions and sauté until golden and almost tender. Add mushrooms and sauté about 5 minutes, stirring constantly; season to taste with salt and pepper. Stir in thyme and cook until mushrooms reduce and become softened.

Reduce heat to medium-low and stir in sherry. Add flour and continue to stir for 3 minutes. Slowly stir in broth. Increase heat to bring soup to a boil, then reduce heat and simmer 10 minutes.

Remove from heat and cool 10 minutes; purée with an immersion blender until smooth. Taste and adjust seasoning. Reheat before serving.

Serve garnished with parsley.

# Cheesy Mushroom Onion Soup

2 tablespoons unsalted butter
2 sweet yellow onions, large chop
kosher salt
freshly ground black pepper
1 pound mushrooms, sliced
3 garlic cloves, minced
3 cups low-sodium chicken broth
3 tablespoons tomato paste
½ teaspoon dried thyme leaves
½ cup good-quality dry white wine
¼ cup minced fresh flat-leaf parsley leaves

½ cup each freshly grated Jarlsberg or Gruyere and Parmesan-Reggiano,
   combined

In a 4-quart saucepan, melt butter over medium-high heat and sauté
onions until soft, seasoning to taste with salt and pepper. Reduce heat to
medium-low, add mushrooms and sauté briefly. Add garlic and cook for
1 minute.

Stir in broth, tomato paste and thyme. Increase heat to bring soup to
a boil, then reduce heat and add wine. Cover and simmer 5 minutes. Stir
in parsley; taste and adjust seasoning.

Ladle soup into bowls and top with the cheeses.

# Roasted Tomato Soup

*Roasting the tomatoes is what gives this soup an amazing depth of flavor. Pair it with a grilled cheese sandwich to enjoy a classic duo.*

4 15-ounce cans chopped tomatoes
3 tablespoons olive oil, divided
kosher salt
fresh ground black pepper
4 ribs celery, diced
2 carrots, diced
1 sweet yellow onion, chopped
4 garlic cloves, minced
2 14-ounce cans low-sodium chicken broth
2 bay leaves
2 tablespoons unsalted butter
½ teaspoon sugar
½ cup chopped fresh basil leaves
kosher salt
freshly ground black pepper

Preheat oven to 450°. Set a mesh strainer over a large bowl. Pour tomatoes in and strain well; reserve tomato liquid. Spread tomatoes onto an aluminum foil-covered large rimmed baking sheet. Drizzle with 1 tablespoon olive oil and season with salt and pepper. Roast for about 40 - 45 minutes, taking care that they do not get too dry.

Meanwhile, heat remaining 2 tablespoons olive oil in a 4-quart saucepan over medium heat. Add celery, carrots and onions; sauté 5 minutes. Lower the heat and cover the pan, cooking vegetables until they are soft.

Remove cover, add garlic and cook 2 minutes. Add reserved liquid, roasted tomatoes, chicken broth, bay leaves, butter and sugar. Bring to a boil, then reduce heat and simmer 20 minutes.

Remove from heat and discard bay leaves; cool 10 minutes. Stir in basil and purée with an immersion blender until smooth. Season to taste with salt and pepper. Reheat before serving.

Flavor improves overnight.

# Minestrone

2 tablespoons olive oil
1 sweet yellow onion, chopped
1 pound carrots, chopped
6 large garlic cloves, minced
2 15-ounce cans petite-cut tomatoes, with liquid
4 14-ounce cans low-sodium chicken broth
15-ounce can white beans (preferably S & W), drained and rinsed
3 ounces tomato paste, or more to your liking
dried oregano
sugar
kosher salt
freshly ground black pepper
1 pound green beans, cut into ½" lengths
9-ounce package fresh cheese tortellini or dried pasta of choice
1 cup frozen petite peas, thawed
dried basil, to taste

Parmesan-Reggiano wedge

In an 8-quart stock pot, heat oil over medium heat and sauté onions and carrots 5 minutes. Cover pot and cook, stirring occasionally, until vegetables are tender. Remove cover and add garlic; cook 2 minutes.

Increase heat to medium-high. Add tomatoes, broth, white beans and tomato paste. When stock is bubbling, add oregano, sugar, salt and pepper, to taste.

Add green beans and cook 5 minutes. Add tortellini, or other pasta, and cook for length of time indicated on package. Add peas and dried basil; heat through.

Serve with freshly grated Parmesan.

# Pasta e Fagioli

2 tablespoons olive oil
2 sweet yellow onions, chopped
1 pound carrots, chopped
6 ribs celery, chopped
6 garlic cloves, minced
4 14-ounce cans low-sodium chicken broth
2 15-ounce cans petite-cut tomatoes, with liquid
2 15-ounce cans white beans (preferably S & W), drained and rinsed
1 tablespoon dried rubbed sage
1 teaspoon dried thyme leaves
kosher salt, to taste
freshly ground black pepper, to taste
¾ cup elbow macaroni

white truffle oil
Parmesan-Reggiano wedge

In an 8-quart stock pot, heat oil over medium heat and sauté onions, carrots and celery for 5 minutes. Cover pan and continue to cook until vegetables are soft. Uncover pan, add garlic and cook 2 minutes.

Add remaining ingredients, except macaroni. Bring to a simmer, covered, and cook 10 minutes. Uncover pan, bring to a boil and stir in macaroni. Simmer until macaroni is cooked through, about
20 minutes.

Pulse a few times with immersion blender to thicken soup.

Ladle into bowls and top with drizzle of truffle oil and freshly grated Parmesan.

# Italian Vegetable Soup

*This is a lighter and quicker version of Minestrone.*

2 tablespoons olive oil
1 small sweet yellow onion, chopped
4 garlic cloves, chopped
2 14-ounce cans low-sodium chicken broth
2 15-ounce cans petite-cut tomatoes, with liquid
1 red bell pepper, diced
½ teaspoon dried basil
½ teaspoon sugar
kosher salt
freshly ground black pepper
½ cup small dried pasta of choice
2 small zucchini, cut lengthwise in quarters and sliced into ¼" pieces
1 cup frozen petite peas, thawed
1 bunch fresh spinach, stems discarded and leaves roughly chopped

Parmesan-Reggiano wedge

In a 4-quart saucepan, heat oil over medium heat and sauté onions until soft. Add garlic and cook 2 minutes.

Add broth and tomatoes; bring to a low boil. Add red peppers and cook until peppers are somewhat softened. Stir in basil and sugar; season to taste with salt and pepper. Add pasta and cook for length of time indicated on package. When pasta is about halfway cooked, stir in zucchini.

When pasta fully cooked, stir in peas and spinach and heat through.

Serve with freshly grated Parmesan.

# Mushroom Barley Soup

¼ cup olive oil
1 sweet yellow onion, chopped
1 pound carrots, chopped
3 celery stalks, chopped
1 pound mushrooms, large dice
¾ cup pearled barley, rinsed
3 garlic cloves, minced
2 tablespoons all-purpose flour
4 14-ounce cans low-sodium chicken or beef broth
15-ounce can petite-size tomatoes, with liquid
2 teaspoons dried thyme leaves
2 teaspoons kosher salt
freshly ground black pepper, to taste
1 tablespoon dry sherry

In an 8-quart stock pot, heat oil over medium heat. Add vegetables and barley and sauté until vegetables are softened, about 25 minutes. Add garlic and cook 3 minutes.

Reduce heat to medium-low and add flour; stir 5 minutes. Increase heat to medium and gradually stir in broth. Add tomatoes and bring soup to a boil, stirring frequently. Reduce heat and hold at an active simmer; stir in seasonings. Cook until barley is tender, about 40 minutes, stirring occasionally. Stir in sherry.

# Mulligatawny

½ cup unsalted butter
1 large sweet yellow onion, chopped
3 stalks celery, chopped
3 carrots, chopped
2 large Granny Smith or other tart apples, peeled and chopped
½ cup all-purpose flour
1½ tablespoons curry powder
4 14-ounce cans low-sodium chicken broth
3 tablespoons tomato paste

In an 8-quart stock pot, melt butter over medium heat and sauté onions, celery and carrots until almost soft. Add apples and cook until all are soft.

Stir in flour and curry; cook for 3 minutes, stirring constantly. Slowly stir in broth and add tomato paste. Simmer, partially covered, for about 40 minutes.

Remove from heat and cool 10 minutes; purée with an immersion blender until smooth. Reheat before serving.

# Chicken Coconut Soup

*This classic Thai soup, known as tom kha gai, has a delicate balance of sweet (sugar), salty (fish sauce), spicy (chile paste) and sour (lime juice). The proportion of ingredients can be easily adjusted to suit your family's palate.*

2 14-ounce cans low-sodium chicken broth
3" piece ginger, peeled and sliced
2 stalks lemongrass, tough outer layers removed; cut into 2" pieces and
   crushed
1 large lime, zested
2 14-ounce cans coconut milk
¼ cup fresh lime juice
3 tablespoons Thai fish sauce
2 tablespoons light brown sugar
1 tablespoon red chile paste
3 chicken tenderloins, thinly sliced horizontally
8 ounces mushrooms, thinly sliced

½ cup chopped cilantro
3 small green chiles, cut in half vertically and very thinly sliced horizontally
3 scallions, thinly sliced

Combine broth, ginger, lemongrass and lime zest in a saucepan. Bring to a boil over medium heat and boil gently for 10 minutes.

Strain broth into a larger saucepan and discard solids. Stir in coconut milk and bring to a simmer. Add lime juice, fish sauce, sugar and chile paste, mixing well. Simmer for 5 minutes. Reduce heat to low and add chicken and mushrooms; cook a few minutes until chicken is cooked through. Taste and adjust balance of flavors.

Ladle into bowls and garnish with cilantro, chiles and scallions.


Suggestion~
For a more substantial soup, add snow peas or chopped bok choy when adding the chicken. Also, consider adding ½ cup steamed white rice to each bowl before ladling in the soup.

# Chicken Soup

*This is the classic "I'm sick and need chicken soup" soup. It may be made in advance and frozen, so when the flu or a cold attacks, comfort is minutes away!*

1 whole chicken
2 yellow onions, halved
8 ribs celery, cut in thirds
1 head garlic, cloves peeled
1 tablespoon kosher salt
1 tablespoon chicken bouillon
½ bunch flat-leaf parsley
bay leaves
2 pounds whole carrots, peeled and cut in half

Place all ingredients, except carrots, in an 8-quart stock pot. Add cold water, filling to within 2" from the top of the pot. Bring to a boil, then reduce to an active simmer, replenishing water as necessary to maintain the level. After
2 hours, skim fat off top.

Add carrots and cook for 30 minutes, or until tender. Remove carrots, rinse and cut ¼" slices; set aside.

Discard the remaining items in the pot. Line a mesh strainer with several layers of cheesecloth and pour soup through the strainer into a large bowl. If need be, repeat straining using fresh cheesecloth. Add the sliced carrots to the broth.

Refrigerate overnight. Skim the fat from the top of bowl and discard. Cook the soup over medium heat for about an hour to further concentrate the flavors. Taste and add more salt, if needed.


Suggestion~
Add matzo balls or egg noodles, of course!

# Cheesy Chicken Chowder with Cauliflower

*A Chemers family favorite since the girls were in elementary school.
I rarely make it really cheesy anymore, but the name has stuck!*

½ cup unsalted butter
1 sweet yellow onion, chopped
1 pound carrots, chopped
½ cup all-purpose flour
4 cups milk, heated
2 14-ounce cans low-sodium chicken broth
2 teaspoons kosher salt
1 teaspoon celery seed
1 teaspoon Worcestershire
1 head cauliflower, cut into very small florets
2 chicken breast halves, cooked and shredded

grated Cheddar cheese

In an 8-quart stock pot, melt butter over medium heat and sauté onions
and carrots for 5 minutes. Cover pan and continue to cook for another
5 minutes.

Remove cover and reduce heat to medium-low. Add flour and cook for
3 minutes, stirring constantly. Slowly stir in the milk and chicken broth.
Raise heat to medium and stir until soup begins to bubble and is somewhat
thickened, about 20 minutes.

Maintain an active simmer; stir in salt, celery seed and Worcestershire. Add
cauliflower and simmer until tender. Reduce heat to low and add shredded
chicken; cook about 5 minutes, or until heated through. Taste and adjust
seasoning.

Top each bowl with some cheese when serving.

# White Corn Tortilla Soup

¼ cup olive oil
4 7" white corn tortillas, cut into 1" squares
1 small yellow onion, chopped
2 jalapenos, minced
4 garlic cloves, minced
16-ounce package frozen white corn, divided
3 15-ounce cans chopped tomatoes, with liquid
2 14-ounce cans low-sodium chicken broth
¼ cup tomato paste
1 tablespoon kosher salt
2½ teaspoons cumin
½ teaspoon chili powder
½ teaspoon sugar
⅛ teaspoon white pepper
2 chicken breast halves, cooked and shredded

In an 8-quart stock pot, heat oil over medium heat. Fry tortilla squares until they begin to crisp and turn golden.

Add onion and jalapeno and cook a few minutes until onion is translucent. Add garlic and cook 2 minutes. Add half the corn and remaining ingredients, except chicken. Bring soup to a low boil; boil for 5 minutes.

Remove from heat and cool 10 minutes; purée with an immersion blender until smooth. Place on medium-low heat, add the remaining corn and heat through. Reduce heat to low and add shredded chicken; cook for 5 minutes, or until heated through. Taste and adjust seasoning.

Suggestion~
When serving, offer any of the following accompaniments:
chopped avocado
lime wedges
chopped fresh cilantro leaves
grated Jack or Cheddar cheese
lightly crushed blue corn tortilla chips

# Chilled Minted Pea Soup

2 tablespoons olive oil
3 - 4 shallots, chopped
2 14-ounce cans low-sodium chicken broth
1½ pounds frozen petite peas, thawed
<1 teaspoon sugar
¼ teaspoon kosher salt
¼ cup roughly chopped fresh mint leaves
freshly ground black pepper, to taste

Heat oil in a 4-quart saucepan over medium-low heat and sauté shallots
until softened. Add broth, peas, sugar and salt. Bring to a boil, then remove
from heat.

Let cool 10 minutes and stir in mint; purée with an immersion blender.
Taste and adjust seasonings.

Refrigerate overnight before serving.


Suggestion~
For a smoother texture, press soup through a mesh strainer or pass through
a food mill.

# Gazpacho

*This is Barry's 'must have' every summer. Laura discovered that using a spicy Bloody Mary mix as a base also gives great results.*

46-ounce bottle V-8 Spicy Hot
2 garlic cloves, minced
1 bunch cilantro, stems discarded and leaves minced
2 English cucumbers, peeled, seeded and diced
2 yellow bell peppers, diced
8 large Roma tomatoes, seeded and diced
1 small red onion, finely diced
½ lemon, juiced
¼ cup olive oil
¼ cup red wine vinegar
2 tablespoons Worcestershire
1½ teaspoons sugar
1 teaspoon dried oregano
½ teaspoon kosher salt
½ teaspoon freshly ground black pepper
1 large avocado, diced

Combine all ingredients, except avocado, in a large bowl. Pulse with an immersion blender until it is the consistency you prefer. Cover and refrigerate overnight.

Taste and adjust seasonings. Stir in avocado before serving.

# Starter and Entrée Salads

Amy's Grapefruit Salad • 52
Fruity Summer Spinach Salad • 53
Mango Mint Salad • 54
Lime Tequila Salad with Chicken • 55
Creamy Caesar Salad with Parmesan Lace • 56
Grilled Vegetable Salad • 58
Balsamic Vinaigrette • 58
Warm Spinach Salad with Poppy Seed Dressing • 59
Warm Orzo Salad with Grilled Shrimp or Chicken • 60
Chinese Chicken Salad • 61
Warm Asian Chicken Spinach Salad • 62
Asian Pasta Salad • 63
Stetson Chopped Salad • 64
Curried Tuna Salad • 65

~

# Amy's Grapefruit Salad

*On one of our trips to southern California to visit family, Laura loved the Amy's salad from Stanley's restaurant in Encino. After that, any time we would visit, she would always request that we go for the salad. This recipe draws its inspiration from Amy's.*

*Vinaigrette:*
3 tablespoons cider vinegar
2½ tablespoons sugar
2 teaspoons dried minced onion
1 teaspoon celery seed
½ teaspoon dried summer savory
½ teaspoon kosher salt
¼ teaspoon dry mustard
¼ cup olive oil

*Salad:*
10-ounce bag butter lettuce
1 large avocado, cut into chunks
¼ small red onion, slivered
2 pink grapefruits, supremed, reserving juice

Place all vinaigrette ingredients, except olive oil, in a container with a lid and shake until well blended. Add oil and shake again. Taste and adjust seasoning. Refrigerate for several hours.

Combine salad ingredients, except grapefruit. Shake vinaigrette container and toss gently with salad, adding reserved juice to taste. Gently toss in grapefruit.

Suggestion~
For a more substantial salad, add cooked and chilled shrimp.

Instructions for grapefruit supremes may be found in Details (page 9).

# Fruity Summer Spinach Salad

*Vinaigrette:*
3 tablespoons raspberry or red wine vinegar
2 tablespoons fresh lime juice
1½ teaspoons sugar
½ teaspoon kosher salt
pinch of dry mustard
pinch of white pepper
1 - 2 tablespoons olive oil

*Salad:*
10-ounce bag spinach, stems discarded and leaves torn
1 avocado, chopped
3 kiwi, sliced and quartered
½ cup blackberries
12 strawberries, sliced
1 orange or yellow bell pepper, thinly sliced
<¼ cup slivered red onion

Whisk all vinaigrette ingredients, except olive oil, in a small bowl. Whisk in oil in a slow stream. Taste and adjust seasoning.

Combine salad ingredients and toss salad with vinaigrette.


Suggestion~
For a more substantial salad, double the vinaigrette and marinate some shrimp in half of it for about 30 minutes; grill.

# Mango Mint Salad

*This salad practically screams summer!*

*Vinaigrette:*
1" piece ginger, roughly chopped
½ ripe mango, diced
3 tablespoons fresh lime juice
3 tablespoons fresh lemon juice
2 tablespoons honey
1 tablespoon Dijon mustard
1 tablespoon low-sodium soy sauce
12 large, fresh mint leaves
½ teaspoon kosher salt
few grindings of black pepper
⅓ cup olive oil

*Salad:*
1½ ripe mangos, cut into chunks
¼ honeydew melon or cantaloupe, cut into small chunks
½ English cucumber, peeled, quartered lengthwise, seeded and sliced
1 avocado, chopped
¼ small red onion, thinly sliced
10-ounce bag red leaf or butter lettuce
¼ cup roughly chopped fresh mint leaves

With food processor running, drop ginger through feed tube to mince. Add remaining vinaigrette ingredients, except oil, to work bowl; process until well blended. Add oil through pusher tube and process until emulsified. Taste and adjust seasoning. Refrigerate in a covered container for several hours.

Combine salad ingredients. Shake vinaigrette container and toss salad with vinaigrette. The extra vinaigrette will keep for a day or two.


Suggestion~
For a more substantial salad, add grilled shrimp or chicken: In a zip-top bag, marinate shelled and deveined shrimp for 1 hour or chicken tenderloins for 2 hours in a little vinaigrette. Discard marinade and grill. Allow to cool before cutting and adding to the salad.

# Lime Tequila Salad with Chicken

*Vinaigrette:*
finely grated zest of 1 lime
3 tablespoons fresh lime juice
1½ tablespoons honey
1 tablespoon tequila
¼ teaspoon kosher salt
¼ teaspoon dried red pepper flakes, or to taste
1 garlic clove, minced
¼ cup olive oil

*Salad:*
1 red bell pepper, quartered
1 yellow bell pepper, quartered
1 jalapeno, halved
1 ear white corn
1 small red onion, ½" slices
10-ounce bag romaine
½ pint cherry or grape tomatoes, halved
1 avocado, cut into chunks
1 - 2 cooked chicken breast halves, shredded

Whisk all vinaigrette ingredients, except oil, in a container with a lid. Whisk in oil in a slow stream. Refrigerate, covered, for several hours.

Grill peppers and jalapeno skin-side down. When the skin is blackened, place them in a plastic bag to steam.

While peppers and jalapeno steam, grill the corn and onion slices. Cut kernels into a salad bowl, then chop the onions, adding them to the bowl. Remove and discard the blackened skin from the peppers and jalapeno. Chop peppers and finely chop jalapeno, adding them to the bowl along with the remaining salad ingredients.

Whisk vinaigrette and spoon onto salad, taking care that pepper flakes, which may settle to the bottom, are added to the salad; toss.

# Creamy Caesar Salad with Parmesan Lace

*My dad made a wicked Caesar when I was growing up. Sadly, he passed away a long time ago and I never got his recipe. What follows isn't done the traditional way using a raw egg yolk as he did, but I think he'd be pleased with the results.*

*Dressing:*
½ cup mayonnaise
½ cup Greek yogurt
½ cup freshly grated Parmesan-Reggiano
1 medium garlic clove, finely minced
>2 tablespoons fresh lemon juice
1 teaspoon Worcestershire
1 teaspoon Dijon mustard
1 teaspoon anchovy paste
½ teaspoon freshly ground black pepper
¼ teaspoon kosher salt

*Salad:*
2 10-ounce bags chopped romaine
½ pint grape or cherry tomatoes, halved

Whisk all dressing ingredients; taste and adjust seasoning. Thin with a bit of water to desired consistency. Cover and refrigerate for several hours.

Toss salad ingredients with dressing. Garnish each serving with Parmesan Lace.


Suggestion~
For a more substantial salad, add any of the following:
1 yellow or orange bell pepper, chopped
½ English cucumber, peeled, seeded and sliced
¼ red onion, thinly sliced
cooked and shredded chicken or thinly sliced cooked steak

# Parmesan Lace

*These are a pleasant change from the predictable croutons typically served in a Caesar... and they are so much prettier.*

½ cup freshly grated Parmesan-Reggiano

Preheat oven to 350°. Cover a cookie sheet with parchment paper. Sprinkle grated cheese, using your fingers or a rotary grater, onto parchment in an even layer just deep enough where the parchment does not show through. Bake about 8 - 10 minutes, or until golden. Slide parchment off the cookie sheet and let lace cool.

Gently break off pieces of lace or crumble it and place atop the salad when serving.


Suggestion~
To incorporate a little kick into the lace, add a bit of cayenne or freshly ground black pepper before baking.

Parmesan lace can also be floated on top of a bowl of tomato soup.

# Grilled Vegetable Salad

*This is our favorite summer salad since we can change it up by using whatever fresh vegetables are available. Given that they'll all be tossed in a vinaigrette, the vegetables don't have to be coated with oil before grilling.*

*Salad possibilities, any or all of the following:*
butter or red leaf lettuce
cherry or grape tomatoes, halved
red/yellow/orange bell peppers, quartered
red onion, cut in ½" slices
asparagus, tough ends broken off and discarded
zucchini, sliced vertically into 4 slices
small eggplant, cut in ¼" vertical slices, discarding the skin ends
scallions
small head radicchio, quartered with core attached
chopped fresh basil leaves
crumbled Feta, crumbled goat cheese or shards of fresh
    Parmesan-Reggiano

Place lettuce and tomatoes in a large salad bowl. Grill peppers skin-side down over high heat until skin is blackened; place in a plastic bag to steam for 5 minutes.

Reduce heat to medium and grill red onion, asparagus and zucchini. Grill eggplant, scallions and radicchio over low heat.

Remove skin from steamed peppers and discard. Chop grilled vegetables to preferred sizes and add to salad with basil and cheese. Toss salad with Balsamic Vinaigrette or vinaigrette of your choice.


# Balsamic Vinaigrette

¼ cup balsamic vinegar
2 teaspoons packed light brown sugar
½ teaspoon kosher salt
½ teaspoon freshly ground black pepper

½ teaspoon Dijon mustard
½ cup, less 1 tablespoon, olive oil

Place all vinaigrette ingredients, except oil, in a container with a lid. Shake well to blend. Add oil and shake again. Taste and adjust seasoning. Refrigerate vinaigrette for several hours before using. Remove from refrigerator 30 minutes before tossing with salad.

# Warm Spinach Salad with Poppy Seed Dressing

*Dressing:*
¼ cup cider vinegar
<¼ cup sugar
1 tablespoon dried minced onion
¾ teaspoon poppy seeds
½ teaspoon dry mustard
½ teaspoon kosher salt
2 tablespoons olive oil
2 tablespoons canola oil

*Salad:*
6 ounces baby spinach leaves, stems discarded and leaves torn
6 ounces sliced mushrooms
6 ounces cherry or grape tomatoes, halved
4 slices bacon, cooked and crumbled or chopped
2 hard-boiled eggs, chopped
¼ red onion, thinly sliced

Place all dressing ingredients, except oils, in a microwaveable bowl; whisk to blend. Add oils in a slow stream, whisking to incorporate. Taste and adjust seasoning; set aside until ready to toss with salad ingredients.

Combine salad ingredients. Warm vinaigrette in the microwave set on High for about 30 seconds. Whisk dressing and toss with salad.

Suggestion~
For a more substantial salad, add cooked and shredded chicken.

# Warm Orzo Salad
# with Grilled Shrimp or Chicken

*Marinade:*
2 garlic cloves, minced
1½ tablespoons fresh lemon juice
¼ cup olive oil
1 teaspoon dried oregano
freshly ground black pepper

12 - 14 U-15 shrimp, shelled and deveined, or 9 chicken tenderloins

*Vinaigrette:*
1 garlic clove, minced
¼ cup fresh lemon juice
1 teaspoon dried oregano
¼ teaspoon kosher salt
freshly ground black pepper, to taste
⅓ cup olive oil

*Salad:*
1½ cups orzo
12 ounces snap peas, cut in half
8 ounces cherry or grape tomatoes, cut in half
6 scallions, thinly sliced
½ cup finely chopped flat-leaf parsley leaves
2 - 4 ounces crumbled Feta

Combine marinade ingredients in a zip-top bag. Add shrimp or chicken and refrigerate 30 minutes for shrimp or 1 hour for chicken.

Place all vinaigrette ingredients, except oil, in a bowl and whisk until well blended. Add oil and whisk again. Taste and adjust seasoning; set aside until ready to add to salad ingredients.

Fill two-thirds of a 3-quart saucepan with water and bring to a boil. Stir in orzo and cook 9 minutes, or until just done. Add snap peas to pan and cook exactly 15 seconds. Drain orzo and peas; transfer to large bowl. Cool 5 minutes.

While pasta and peas are cooling, drain shrimp or chicken, discarding marinade, and grill. Add remaining salad ingredients and vinaigrette to warm orzo. Cut shrimp or chicken into bite-size pieces and stir into salad; serve immediately.

# Chinese Chicken Salad

*This favorite, with its light and fresh flavor, is adapted from Comforts' restaurant in San Anselmo.*

*Vinaigrette:*
1 garlic clove, minced
⅓ cup unseasoned rice vinegar (preferably Marukan)
¼ cup sugar
1½ teaspoons kosher salt
1 teaspoon freshly ground black pepper
3 ounces canola oil
2 teaspoons sesame oil

*Salad:*
10-ounce bag romaine lettuce, roughly chopped
10-ounce bag iceberg lettuce, roughly chopped
8 scallions, thinly sliced
1 red bell pepper, thinly sliced and cut in thirds
1 yellow or orange bell pepper, thinly sliced and cut in thirds
½ cucumber, peeled, seeded and thinly sliced
2 cooked chicken breast halves, shredded
¼ cup slivered almonds, toasted
4 oranges, peeled, sliced and large chop; reserving juice

Place all vinaigrette ingredients, except oils, in a container with a lid and shake until well blended. Add oils and shake again. Taste and adjust seasoning. Refrigerate for several hours.

Combine salad ingredients, except oranges. Shake vinaigrette container and toss salad with vinaigrette, taking care that garlic, which may settle to the bottom, is added. Toss in oranges and reserved juice.

# Warm Asian Chicken Spinach Salad

*Marinade:*
½ cup low-sodium soy sauce
2 tablespoons sugar
1 tablespoon grated fresh ginger
2 garlic cloves, minced

6 chicken tenderloins

*Vinaigrette:*
¼ cup ketchup
¼ cup unseasoned rice vinegar (preferably Marukan)
1 tablespoon sugar
1½ teaspoons canola oil
a couple dashes Tabasco
1½ teaspoons sesame oil

*Salad:*
10-ounce bag spinach leaves, stems discarded and leaves torn
1 orange bell pepper, thinly sliced
6 ounces mushrooms, sliced
¼ red onion, thinly sliced
6 ounces cherry or grape tomatoes, halved
1 tablespoon sesame seeds, toasted

Combine marinade ingredients in zip-top bag. Add chicken and refrigerate for a few hours. When ready to put the salad together, remove marinated chicken and drain marinade into a small saucepan.

Whisk all vinaigrette ingredients, except sesame oil, in the saucepan with the marinade. Bring to a boil and boil 5- 7 minutes. Remove from heat, stir in sesame oil and set aside to cool a bit.

Grill marinated chicken and cut into bite-size pieces. Combine salad ingredients, add grilled chicken and toss all with the warm vinaigrette.


Suggestion~
The grilled chicken may be substituted with grilled steak.

# Asian Pasta Salad

*Vinaigrette:*
2 small garlic cloves
2 tablespoons honey
1 tablespoon dry mustard
2 teaspoons peanut butter
½ teaspoon ground ginger
½ cup low-sodium soy sauce
2 teaspoons sesame oil
½ cup unseasoned rice vinegar (preferably Marukan)
½ teaspoon kosher salt
freshly ground black pepper, to taste
⅓ cup canola oil

*Salad:*
16-ounce box thin spaghetti
½ pound snap peas, cut in quarters
1 red bell pepper, diced
1 yellow bell pepper, diced
4 carrots, grated
4 scallions, thinly sliced
2 cooked chicken breast halves, shredded
1 tablespoon sesame seeds, toasted

~

With food processor running, drop garlic through feed tube to mince. Add remaining vinaigrette ingredients, except canola oil, to work bowl. Process until well blended. Add oil through pusher tube and process until emulsified. Transfer vinaigrette to a large bowl.

Break spaghetti in half and cook per package directions. Add snap peas the last 15 seconds of cooking. Drain spaghetti and snap peas; do not rinse.

Combine spaghetti, snap peas and remaining salad ingredients, except sesame seeds, with the vinaigrette, stirring occasionally while it cools; refrigerate at least 6 hours. When ready to serve, bring to room temperature and toss in sesame seeds.

# Stetson Chopped Salad

*This unusual and flavorful salad is an adaptation from Cowboy Ciao in Scottsdale. As the name suggests, the restaurant has quite an eclectic menu.*

*Dressing:*
¼ cup mayonnaise
2 tablespoons Greek yogurt
½ cup buttermilk
¼ cup pesto
1 small shallot, finely minced
2 teaspoons fresh lemon juice
kosher salt, to taste
freshly ground black pepper, to taste

*Salad:*
1¼ cups water
½ teaspoon kosher salt
1 teaspoon olive oil
1 cup pearl couscous
2 cups packed roughly chopped arugula
4 ounces smoked salmon, chopped
¾ cup quartered cherry or grape tomatoes
1 yellow or orange bell pepper, diced
⅓ cup grated Asiago cheese
¼ cup pepitas
¼ cup dried sweet corn
3 tablespoons dried black currants

Whisk all dressing ingredients together and refrigerate a couple of hours.

Bring water to a boil and add salt, oil and couscous; cover pan. Reduce heat and simmer for 8 - 10 minutes, stirring occasionally. Transfer couscous to a large bowl and stir occasionally as it cools to keep it from clumping together. When completely cooled, add remaining salad ingredients and toss with enough dressing to moisten well.

Suggestion~
The smoked salmon may be substituted with cooked and flaked salmon or cooked and shredded chicken.

# Curried Tuna Salad

*This is an unexpected twist on a classic.*

½ cup mayonnaise + more if desired
1 teaspoon curry powder, or to taste
12-ounce can solid white albacore tuna packed in water, drained and
   chopped
½ Granny Smith apple, diced
½ cup toasted and chopped walnuts
2 - 3 tablespoons finely sliced scallions or minced red onion
2 tablespoons currants

Combine mayonnaise and curry. Add remaining ingredients and refrigerate
for several hours.

# Entrées

Simple Marinara • 69
Linguine with Roasted Tomatoes and Garlic • 70
Tortellini with Artichoke Sauce • 71
Rio Grill Pasta • 72
Linguine with Tomato and Goat Cheese Sauce • 73
Pasta del Magnifico • 74
Fettuccine with Asparagus and Cannellini • 75
Spinach Lasagna • 76
Portobello and Onion Pasta • 78
Roasted Mushroom Risotto • 79
Autumnal Vegetable Stew • 80
Curried Vegetable Stew • 81
Lemon Fish • 82
Breaded Fish • 83
South-of-the-Border Red Snapper • 84
Asian-Style Salmon Patties • 85
Honey and Soy Salmon • 86
Sweet and Spicy Grilled Salmon • 87
Shrimp Cakes with Red Pepper Coulis • 88
Grilled Shrimp with Feta, Tomatoes and Angel Hair • 90
Shrimp Creole • 91
Shrimp Pad Thai • 92
Shrimp Scampi • 94
Fettuccine with Scallops • 95
Crispy Chicken • 96
Baked "Fried" Chicken • 97
Chicken Pizza • 98
Honey Pistachio Chicken • 99

*Continued…*

~

# Simple Marinara

*This marinara is not only quick and easy to make, it's full of flavor and versatile as well.*

2 tablespoons olive oil
1 small sweet yellow onion, chopped
2 garlic cloves, minced
2 15-ounce cans diced tomatoes, drained
½ teaspoon dried oregano
½ teaspoon dried basil
¼ teaspoon sugar
pinch dried red pepper flakes
kosher salt, to taste
freshly ground black pepper, to taste
½ pound pasta of choice, cooked

Parmesan-Reggiano wedge

Heat oil in a skillet and sauté onions over medium heat until soft. Add garlic and cook 2 minutes.

Stir in tomatoes and, when hot, add seasonings; simmer for 20 minutes. Taste and adjust seasoning. Toss with freshly cooked pasta.

Serve with a generous grating of Parmesan.


Suggestion~
If a smooth rather than a chunky marinara is preferred, use a potato masher to crush the tomatoes after they have cooked for about 20 minutes, mashing them until they are the desired consistency.

Add any of the following:
sliced sun-dried tomatoes
diced red peppers
sautéed mushrooms
cooked shrimp or cooked and shredded chicken
a couple of tablespoons tomato paste - for a heartier sauce
15-ounce can cannellini or white beans, drained and rinsed
fresh mozzarella cubes - add right before serving

# Linguine with Roasted Tomatoes and Garlic

2 pounds cherry or grape tomatoes, halved
6 large garlic cloves, unpeeled
olive oil
kosher salt
freshly ground black pepper
9-ounce package fresh linguine
¼ cup loosely-packed chopped basil

Parmesan-Reggiano wedge

Preheat oven to 400°. Place tomatoes and garlic cloves on a large rimmed baking sheet, drizzle with olive oil to coat lightly and season with salt and pepper, tossing gently. Arrange tomatoes cut-side up; roast for about 35 minutes, taking care that tomatoes do not get too dry.

When tomatoes and garlic are done, let cool for about 10 minutes. When garlic is cool enough to handle, cut stem ends off the cloves. Press each clove with the side of a knife to extrude the garlic; set aside.

In a 3-quart saucepan, bring water to a boil and cook pasta according to package directions. When pasta is done, dip a measuring cup in the pasta water and remove ⅓ cup; drain pasta. Reduce heat to low and place the saucepan back on the burner, adding the reserved pasta water and pasta; toss and season to taste with salt and pepper. Gently toss in the tomatoes, garlic and basil.

Serve with a generous grating of Parmesan.

# Tortellini with Artichoke Sauce

*Any chunky-shaped pasta would work well with this sauce if you don't prefer tortellini.*

2 6-ounce jars artichokes marinated in oil (preferably Cara Mia)
1 small sweet yellow onion, chopped
½ teaspoon dried oregano
½ teaspoon dried basil
½ teaspoon kosher salt
¼ teaspoon freshly ground black pepper
pinch dried red pepper flakes
2 large garlic cloves, minced
2 15-ounce cans chopped tomatoes, drained
½ teaspoon sugar
9-ounce package fresh cheese tortellini, cooked

Parmesan-Reggiano wedge

Drain oil from one jar of artichokes into a skillet; set artichokes aside. Sauté onions in artichoke oil over medium-low heat. When onions begin to soften, add seasonings. Continue cooking until onions are tender. Add garlic and cook 2 minutes.

Stir in tomatoes and sugar; simmer for 20 minutes. Drain and discard oil from second jar of artichokes. Rough chop artichokes and add to tomato sauce; heat through. Taste and adjust seasonings. Gently stir in freshly cooked tortellini.

Serve with a generous grating of Parmesan.

# Rio Grill Pasta

*On a vacation in Carmel many years ago, we went to Rio Grill and had this fabulously flavorful pasta dish. You can only imagine how excited we were when we saw the recipe published in our hotel's magazine! What follows was inspired by that visit.*

14-ounce can low-sodium chicken or vegetable broth
3 tablespoons balsamic vinegar
2 tablespoons olive oil (omit if sun-dried tomatoes are oil-packed)
2 tablespoons fresh lemon juice
1 large garlic clove, minced
<½ teaspoon dried red pepper flakes
8-ounce package frozen artichokes hearts, thawed and sliced
1 red, orange or yellow pepper, sliced
⅓ cup sun-dried tomatoes, sliced
9-ounce package fresh fettuccine, cooked very al dente
½ bunch spinach leaves, stems discarded

Parmesan-Reggiano wedge

Place broth, vinegar, oil, lemon juice, garlic and pepper flakes in a skillet. Bring to a boil, then lower heat and reduce to a simmer. Add artichokes, peppers and tomatoes; cook for 5 - 7 minutes.

Stir in fettuccine and let stand a few minutes to allow some liquid to absorb into it. Add the spinach leaves and stir until just wilted.

Serve in bowls with a generous grating of Parmesan.


Suggestion~
The top edge of the artichoke can be tough, so trim accordingly.

# Linguine with Tomato and Goat Cheese Sauce

*This is a good choice for a summer pasta dish; it uses fresh tomatoes and presents a light sauce that just barely cooks.*

2 pounds tomatoes, seeded and cut into large dice
kosher salt
4 ounces goat cheese, room temperature
2 tablespoons olive oil, divided
¼ teaspoon dried red pepper flakes
9-ounce package fresh linguine
2 garlic cloves, minced
½ cup loosely-packed julienned basil

Place tomatoes in a colander set over a bowl and lightly salt. Let stand 20 minutes to drain, stirring occasionally; reserve liquid and set aside.

In a small bowl, mash cheese with 1 tablespoon oil and red pepper flakes; set aside.

Cook pasta according to package directions and drain. While pasta is draining, reduce heat to low and, using the same pan, add the reserved liquid, remaining 1 tablespoon oil and the garlic to warm. Add the cheese mixture, stirring until melted. Add tomatoes and gently stir until warmed through. Stir in basil and toss with pasta.


Suggestion~
If fresh tomatoes are unavailable, substitute with 4 15-ounce cans diced tomatoes.

# Pasta del Magnifico

*When Julia spent a semester in Florence, she and her roommate became friends with Guilliano, the owner of La Cucina del Garga. They spent many nights there and raved about the food and the company. When Barry and I visited her, dining at Garga was one of the most memorable experiences of the trip. This is one of their signature dishes, and while it doesn't come with amiable Italian waiters and candlelight, it certainly is magnifico. Cincin!*

1 cup heavy cream
1 large lemon, zested
1 large navel orange, zested
2 tablespoons cognac or dry sherry
½ teaspoon kosher salt
3 tablespoons chopped fresh mint
15 large basil leaves, chopped
9-ounce package fresh linguine
½ cup freshly grated Parmesan-Reggiano

Heat cream in a skillet over medium-low heat. When warmed, stir in zest, liqueur and salt. Bring cream to a simmer and simmer for about 7 minutes.

While cream is heating and simmering, bring water to a boil for pasta. Cook pasta according to package directions and drain.

When cream has simmered, stir in herbs. Using tongs, add pasta to the cream, then sprinkle in the Parmesan, moving the pasta around for about a minute to coat evenly. Serve immediately in warmed bowls or plates.


Suggestion~
For a more substantial dish, top the pasta with sautéed shrimp or seared sea scallops.

# Fettuccine with Asparagus and Cannellini

2 tablespoons olive oil
1 pound asparagus, cut into 1" pieces diagonally
1 tablespoon minced garlic
15-ounce can diced tomatoes, drained
15-ounce can cannellini or white beans (preferably S & W), drained and
   rinsed
1 teaspoon dried Italian seasoning
1 cup low-sodium chicken or vegetable broth
kosher salt
freshly ground black pepper
9-ounce package fresh fettuccine, cooked

Parmesan-Reggiano wedge

Heat oil in a large skillet over medium heat and sauté asparagus for a few
minutes until they begin to soften. Add garlic and cook 1 minute.

Stir in tomatoes, beans, Italian seasoning and broth. Season to taste with
salt and pepper. Bring to a boil; reduce to an active simmer until mixture
thickens. Toss with freshly cooked pasta.

Serve with a generous grating of Parmesan.

# Spinach Lasagna

*Lasagna is always labor-intensive, which can make it an intimidating dish for some. However, making the sauce one day and then assembling it another day can make it much more manageable... and the effort is worth it!*

*Sauce:*
1 tablespoon olive oil
1 large sweet yellow onion, chopped
6 garlic cloves, minced
4 15-ounce cans chopped tomatoes, drained
12-ounce can tomato paste
¼ cup finely chopped flat-leaf parsley
1½ teaspoon dried oregano
1 teaspoon dried basil
½ teaspoon sugar
kosher salt, to taste
freshly ground black pepper, to taste
1 bay leaf

11 lasagna noodles

*Filling:*
2 large eggs
16-ounce container ricotta
½ cup freshly grated Parmesan-Reggiano
10-ounce package frozen chopped spinach, thawed and squeezed dry
8 ounces grated mozzarella

Parmesan-Reggiano or Pecorino wedge

Heat oil in a large skillet over medium heat and sauté onions until soft. Add garlic and cook 2 minutes. Stir in remaining sauce ingredients and simmer 40 minutes; discard bay leaf. Let cool to room temperature.

Cook lasagna noodles according to package directions. Drain and lay noodles on paper towels, patting the top of the noodles dry with a paper towel.

Preheat oven to 350°. In a large bowl, beat the eggs. Add ricotta and Parmesan, stirring until well blended. Add spinach and mozzarella, combining well. To assemble, follow layering on the next page.

In a 9" x 13" baking pan, layer from *bottom to top:*
• smear of sauce
• 3 noodles
• ½ the spinach-cheese mixture
• ½ the sauce
• 5 noodles, cut to 8½" and laid perpendicularly to full-length noodles
• remaining spinach-cheese mixture
• 3 noodles
• remaining sauce

Cover with aluminum foil and bake for 1 hour. Discard foil and bake an additional 15 minutes. Cool 15 minutes before cutting. Generously grate fresh Parmesan or Pecorino over before serving.


Suggestion~
If meat lasagna is preferred, omit spinach and arrange 2 cooked and crumbled mild or hot Italian sausages on top of the middle layer of sauce.

May be frozen before baking. Wrap well in plastic wrap, then aluminum foil. Thaw in the refrigerator for 3 days and remove it from the refrigerator 2 hours before baking.

# Portobello and Onion Pasta

*This creamy sauce with mushrooms and caramelized onions is just divine!*

5 tablespoons butter, divided
1 tablespoon sugar
1 large red onion, sliced
kosher salt
freshly ground black pepper
2 tablespoons olive oil
2 large leeks, white and light green part only, sliced
4 portobello mushrooms, gills scraped and large chop
½ teaspoon dried thyme leaves
3 tablespoons dry white wine
2 ounces goat cheese, room temperature
8 ounces gemelli or rotini, cooked; reserve about ½ cup pasta water right
   before draining

In a skillet, melt 3 tablespoons butter over medium-high heat and add sugar, stirring until dissolved. Add red onions and sauté about 15 minutes, seasoning to taste with salt and pepper. Transfer to a small bowl and set aside.

Reduce heat to medium-low and add remaining 2 tablespoons butter and the oil to the pan, scraping any residue on the bottom. When butter is melted, add leeks and cook until limp. Add portobellos and cook until partially softened. Stir in thyme and season to taste with salt and pepper. Sauté until portobellos are cooked through.

Stir in reserved onions and wine and sauté until vegetables are tender. Add cheese, stirring until melted. Pour in some of the reserved pasta water, a little at a time, until a creamy consistency is reached. Add freshly cooked pasta and heat through.

# Roasted Mushroom Risotto

1 pound mushrooms, sliced
olive oil
kosher salt, to taste
freshly ground black pepper, to taste
2 14-ounce cans low-sodium chicken broth
2 tablespoons butter
1 small sweet yellow onion, chopped
¾ cup Arborio rice
½ cup dry white wine
½ cup freshly grated Parmesan-Reggiano

white truffle oil

Preheat oven to 400°. Place mushrooms on a large rimmed baking sheet and toss with enough oil to coat. Arrange in an even layer and season with salt and pepper. Roast for about 35 - 40 minutes, or until very soft. While mushrooms are roasting, begin the risotto.

Heat chicken stock to an active simmer and hold simmering.

Melt butter in a 3-quart saucepan over medium heat and add onions; cook until soft, seasoning with salt and pepper. Add rice, stirring for 2 minutes to coat grains with butter.

Add wine and stir continuously until it is mostly absorbed. Ladle in 1 cup broth and stir continuously until broth is mostly absorbed. Continue ladling broth in 1-cup increments until most of broth is used. Taste rice for texture; it should be al dente. Taste and adjust seasoning.

When the rice is to your liking and broth is almost absorbed, turn off heat and gently stir in mushrooms and Parmesan. Serve immediately in heated bowls and top with a light drizzle of truffle oil.


Suggestion~
For a more substantial risotto, add at the end of cooking:
½ cup frozen petite peas, thawed
1 cooked and shredded chicken breast

# Autumnal Vegetable Stew

2 tablespoons olive oil
2 red onions, large dice
2 pounds butternut squash, large dice
1 red pepper, large dice
1 orange or yellow pepper, large dice
dried thyme leaves
dried rubbed sage
kosher salt
freshly ground black pepper
6 large garlic cloves, minced
3 14-ounce cans low-sodium chicken broth
1 large Granny Smith, or other tart apple, peeled and diced
⅓ cup uncooked white rice

Heat oil in a stock pot over medium-high heat. Add onions, squash, peppers, herbs and seasoning, to taste. Cook, stirring frequently, about 15 minutes. Reduce heat to medium-low and add garlic; cook 4 minutes stirring frequently.

Raise heat to medium-high and add broth. Bring broth to a boil, then reduce to an active simmer. Cook about 20 minutes or until squash is just tender.

Add apples and rice; cook 30 minutes, or until rice is tender. Taste and adjust seasoning.


Suggestion~
If you prefer a more substantial stew, add 1 or 2 cooked and shredded chicken breasts at the end of cooking; cook until heated through.

# Curried Vegetable Stew

3 garlic cloves
1" piece chopped fresh ginger
3 tablespoons water
1 tablespoon canola oil
3 small sweet yellow onions, chopped
1 tablespoon curry powder
½ teaspoon cumin
15-ounce can low-sodium chicken or vegetable broth
15-ounce can crushed tomatoes
½ teaspoon kosher salt
¼ teaspoon freshly ground black pepper
¼ teaspoon ground cinnamon
1 medium sweet potato, peeled and large dice
1 small cauliflower, cut into bite-size florets
3 medium zucchini, large dice
1 cup frozen petite peas, thawed
¼ cup currants

cooked couscous

In a food processor work bowl, purée garlic, ginger and water until smooth; set aside.

Heat oil in a stock pot over medium-high heat and sauté onions until soft. Add curry and cumin, cook for 1 minute.

Stir in the garlic-ginger purée and cook an additional minute. Add broth, tomatoes, salt, pepper and cinnamon; stir well. Increase heat and bring to boil, then reduce to an active simmer. Simmer for about 10 minutes.

Add potatoes and cauliflower, cover and simmer 20 minutes, stirring periodically. Mix in zucchini, peas and currants. Simmer, covered, for an additional 20 minutes, or until vegetables are tender, stirring periodically.

Serve stew on a bed of couscous.


Suggestion~
If you prefer a more substantial stew, add 1 or 2 cooked and shredded chicken breasts at the end of cooking; cook until heated through.

# Lemon Fish

3 slices buttermilk, potato or other 'light' bread
½ teaspoon kosher salt
1 egg
4 tilapia fillets, or similar fish
2 tablespoons unsalted butter, melted
1 tablespoon fresh lemon juice

lemon wedges

Preheat oven to 400°. Tear bread into small pieces and place in the work bowl of a food processor; pulse to create bread crumbs. Transfer crumbs to a pie plate and toss with salt. In a separate pie plate, beat the egg.

Dip fish, one at a time, first in the egg, then in the bread crumbs. Place in a 9" x 13" baking pan sprayed with cooking spray.

Combine butter and lemon juice; drizzle over fish. Cook for 20 minutes.

Serve with lemon wedges.


Suggestion~
A very thin fish, such as sole, may also be used; fold it in half when placing it in the pan.

# Breaded Fish

¼ cup plain bread crumbs
½ cup panko
1 teaspoon kosher salt
freshly ground black pepper, to taste
4 large tilapia fillets, or similar fish
⅓ cup mayonnaise + more, if needed
½ lemon, juiced
1½ tablespoons unsalted butter, melted
Parmesan-Reggiano wedge

lemon wedges

Preheat oven to 400°. Combine bread crumbs, panko, salt and pepper in a pie plate.

Taking one fillet at a time, use the back of a spoon to smear one side of fish with mayonnaise; press the mayonnaise side into the crumbs. Repeat on the other side. Place fish in a 9" x 13" baking pan sprayed with cooking spray. Repeat with remaining fish.

Combine lemon juice and butter; spoon over fish and cook 15 minutes. Grate a generous amount of Parmesan over fillets and cook for an additional 5 minutes.

Serve with lemon wedges.

# South~of~the~Border Red Snapper

2 garlic cloves, minced
1 teaspoon kosher salt
2 pounds red snapper fillets
¼ cup fresh lime juice
¼ cup olive oil, divided
1 sweet yellow onion, sliced very thinly
2 15-ounce cans petite-cut tomatoes, drained
2 jalapenos, minced
¼ teaspoon dried oregano
3 bay leaves
kosher salt
freshly ground black pepper
¼ cup chopped cilantro
2 tablespoons unsalted butter

Place garlic and salt in a small bowl. Using a fork, mash them together to create a paste; rub paste over the fish. Place in a zip-top bag, add lime juice and marinate for 2 hours.

Heat 2 tablespoons oil in a skillet over medium heat and sauté onions about 5 minutes. Add tomatoes, jalapenos, oregano and bay leaves; simmer about 15 minutes; season with salt and pepper, to taste. Discard bay leaves and stir in cilantro. Transfer tomato-onion mixture to a bowl and keep warm.

Add remaining 2 tablespoons oil and the butter to the same pan. When butter is sizzling, but not brown, add fish. Cook on each side until done. Top with tomato-onion mixture.

# Asian~Style Salmon Patties

1-pound salmon fillet, skinned
kosher salt
freshly ground black pepper
2 eggs
1 garlic clove, minced
1 tablespoon grated fresh ginger
3 scallions, thinly sliced
3 tablespoons hoisin sauce + more for topping patties
¾ teaspoon kosher salt
freshly ground black pepper, to taste
¾ cup panko
6 tablespoons canola oil, divided

Preheat oven to 400°. Place salmon on a foil-lined baking sheet sprayed with cooking spray and season with salt and pepper; cook for 15 minutes. Lift foil off the baking sheet and let salmon cool for 10 minutes; refrigerate for 30 minutes.

In a bowl, beat eggs and combine with remaining ingredients, except oil. Break up salmon into 1" pieces and combine with egg mixture. Form into 4 or 6 patties (depending on the size you prefer) and chill for 30 minutes.

Heat 3 tablespoons oil in a large skillet over medium-high heat and, when oil is hot, cook 2 or 3 patties on each side for about 3 - 4 minutes. Transfer to plate and keep warm. Wipe out skillet with paper towels and repeat with remaining oil and patties.

Top each patty with a bit of hoisin sauce when serving.

# Honey and Soy Salmon

¼ cup honey
¼ cup low-sodium soy sauce
¼ cup fresh lime juice
2 large garlic cloves, minced
4 salmon fillets, skinned
kosher salt
freshly ground black pepper

In a small saucepan, whisk soy sauce, honey, lime juice and garlic. Bring to a boil over medium heat, then reduce to an active simmer. Simmer until the liquid reduces, about 10 - 15 minutes. Remove from heat and let cool to room temperature.

When sauce is cool, preheat oven to 400°. Place salmon on a foil-lined baking sheet sprayed with cooking spray and season with salt and pepper; cook for 20 minutes. Spoon some of the sauce over each fillet when serving.

# Sweet and Spicy Grilled Salmon

*Laura's favorite summer salmon!*

1 tablespoon butter
2 medium shallots, finely chopped
¼ cup fresh lemon juice
3 tablespoons brown sugar
<⅛ teaspoon cayenne
1 tablespoon grated fresh ginger
¼ cup red wine vinegar
3 tablespoons low-sodium soy sauce
3 salmon fillets, skinned

In a small saucepan, melt butter over medium heat and sauté shallots until softened. Add remaining ingredients, except salmon, and stir until well blended; remove from heat.

Grill salmon, basting liberally with sauce. Spoon extra sauce over salmon when serving.

# Shrimp Cakes
# with Red Pepper Coulis

*The beauty of this dish, other than its taste, is that it may be made ahead, frozen, and reheated when needed. If you're serving more than four people (I usually serve 2 per person), the convenience of making it ahead really pays off.*

1½ pounds shrimp, peeled and deveined
3 shallots, finely chopped
1 red pepper, finely chopped
½ teaspoon dried tarragon, crushed
3 tablespoons mayonnaise
3 egg whites
¾ cup bread crumbs or panko
1½ tablespoons capers
¾ teaspoon kosher salt
freshly ground black pepper
4 tablespoons butter, divided

Place shrimp in a food processor work bowl and use the pulse button to chop the shrimp until chunky. Transfer to a bowl and add remaining ingredients, except butter; blend well with a fork. Form the mixture into eight cakes. Cover and refrigerate several hours before cooking.

Melt 2 tablespoons butter in a large skillet over medium heat. Fry four of the cakes until golden, about 5 minutes per side; transfer to paper towels.

Wipe out pan with a paper towel and repeat with the remaining four cakes. Serve shrimp cakes immediately napped in the Red Pepper Coulis.

Suggestion~
If making ahead and freezing, place the cooled cakes on a cookie sheet and freeze for 45 minutes. Wrap them well in plastic wrap, then aluminum foil and place them into a freezer zip-top bag. Reheat by placing frozen cakes on an aluminum foil-lined cookie sheet. Bake for 20 minutes at 375°, turning over halfway through baking.

# Red Pepper Coulis

2 tablespoons olive oil
1 small sweet yellow onion, diced
1½ red peppers, diced
2 garlic cloves, minced
½ cup good-quality dry white wine
1 cup low-sodium chicken broth
pinch kosher salt

In a small saucepan, heat oil over medium heat and sauté onions and red peppers until soft. Add garlic and cook 2 minutes. Deglaze the pan with wine and add chicken broth; bring to a simmer and cook for 15 minutes.

Remove from heat and let cool 10 minutes. Purée with immersion blender; taste and adjust seasoning. Reheat before serving.


Suggestion~
Coulis may be made ahead and frozen. Thaw overnight in the refrigerator.

# Grilled Shrimp with Feta, Tomatoes and Angel Hair

3 ounces olive oil
¼ cup fresh lime juice
3 large garlic cloves, minced
2 tablespoons chopped cilantro leaves, divided
10 U-15 shrimp, peeled and deveined
6 small tomatoes, seeded and chopped
2 ½"-thick slices red onion
2 ounces crumbled Feta
¼ teaspoon dried red pepper flakes, or to taste
8 ounces angel hair, cooked

In a zip-top bag, mix oil, lime juice and garlic with 1 tablespoon cilantro. Add shrimp and marinate at room temperature 30 minutes.

Place tomatoes in a strainer and lightly salt; set aside, stirring occasionally until ready to use.

Drain marinade into a small saucepan and bring to a boil. Boil several minutes; reduce heat to medium-low and cook an additional 5 minutes. Remove from heat.

Grill onions. Add remaining 1 tablespoon cilantro, Feta and red pepper flakes to the sauce. When onions are grilled, chop and add to the sauce.

Grill shrimp. While shrimp are grilling, toss pasta with sauce and plate. Place shrimp on top of pasta and sprinkle with chopped tomatoes.

# Shrimp Creole

*I love having this in my repertoire for when I don't have a lot of time to put something together for dinner, but still want something substantial and delicious.*

4 tablespoons butter
1 medium yellow onion, diced
3 garlic cloves, minced
3 tablespoons all-purpose flour
1 teaspoon kosher salt
¼ teaspoon freshly ground black pepper
1½ teaspoons chili powder
2 15-ounce cans chopped tomatoes, with liquid
few dashes Tabasco
1 red pepper, chopped
½ green pepper, chopped
1 pound shrimp, peeled, deveined and cut bite-size, if large
¼ cup minced flat-leaf parsley leaves

steamed white rice

In a large skillet, melt butter over medium heat and sauté onions until soft. Add garlic and cook for a minute or two. Lower heat and add flour and seasonings. Cook 3 minutes, stirring constantly.

Increase heat to medium; add tomatoes and Tabasco. Cook until thickened, stirring constantly. Reduce heat to an active simmer.

Stir in peppers and cook until almost soft. Add shrimp and cook until shrimp are opaque in the center. Remove from heat and stir in parsley. Taste and adjust seasoning.

Serve on a bed of rice.

# Shrimp Pad Thai

*My sister, Linda, inspired this flavorful dish.*

8 ounces rice noodles

*Marinade:*
¼ cup warm water
1 tablespoon tamarind paste
¼ cup dark brown sugar
3 tablespoons fish sauce
1 teaspoon hot chili sauce, or more to taste
1 pound shrimp, peeled, deveined and cut bite-size, if large

*Stir-fry:*
3 tablespoons peanut or canola oil, divided
2 cups shredded green cabbage
½ cup shredded carrots
4 shallots, thinly sliced
2 garlic cloves, minced
2 eggs, beaten
½ cup minced cilantro leaves
6 scallions, light green and white part only, thinly sliced on an angle

roasted peanuts, crushed
lime wedges

Hydrate noodles, according to package directions, while prepping ingredients.

In a small bowl, combine water and tamarind paste. Add brown sugar, fish sauce and chili sauce. Place shrimp in a zip-top bag with enough of the sauce to coat the shrimp; marinate for 20 minutes. Set remaining sauce aside.

Drain noodles and set aside. Heat 1½ tablespoons oil in a wok or large skillet over medium-high heat. When hot, add shrimp and stir-fry until they are almost cooked through; transfer to a bowl and set aside.

Add remaining 1½ tablespoons oil and stir-fry cabbage, carrots, shallots and garlic until vegetables are limp. Move vegetables to the sides of pan and add eggs. Lightly scramble them, incorporating them into the vegetables.

Add noodles and remaining sauce, tossing to combine well. Cover pan and allow the sauce to boil and absorb into the noodles for about 2 minutes. Return
shrimp to the pan and toss to combine. Turn off heat and stir in cilantro and scallions.

Serve sprinkled with peanuts on top and lime wedges on the side.


Suggestion~
Stir-frying is a very fast cooking method, so it is essential to have everything prepped and within reach before the cooking begins. Once the first item of food is in the pan, stir continuously until everything is cooked.

If tamarind paste is unavailable, lime juice or white vinegar may be used as a substitute.

# Shrimp Scampi

4 tablespoons unsalted butter, divided
2 tablespoons olive oil
3 cloves garlic, minced
pinch dried red pepper flakes
¾ pound U-20 shrimp, peeled and deveined
kosher salt
freshly ground black pepper
½ cup dry white wine
2 tablespoons fresh lemon juice
¼ cup chopped flat-leaf parsley leaves
9-ounce package fresh linguine, cooked al dente

In a large skillet, melt 2 tablespoons butter in oil over medium heat. Add garlic and red pepper flakes; stir for one minute. Add shrimp and season them with salt and pepper. Sauté shrimp until almost cooked through. Transfer to a bowl and set aside.

Add wine and lemon juice to the skillet and bring to a boil, then reduce heat to medium-low. When sauce has cooled a bit, add remaining 2 tablespoons butter, stirring until melted. Return shrimp to the skillet and add parsley and pasta. Toss all together for another minute or two, or until the shrimp are cooked through and the pasta has absorbed much of the sauce.

Suggestion~
While it goes against tradition, topping the dish with a seeded and diced tomato adds color, texture and flavor.

# Fettuccine with Scallops

*The combination of the heat from the red pepper flakes and the sweet from the seared scallops is balanced with the acidity from the lemon, creating a wonderful flavor.*

2½ tablespoons unsalted butter, divided
2 tablespoons olive oil, divided
1 pound asparagus, cut into 1" pieces diagonally
1 red pepper, sliced vertically into ¼" strips and cut crosswise in thirds
1 orange pepper, sliced vertically into ¼" strips and cut crosswise in thirds
2 large garlic cloves, minced
<½ teaspoon dried red pepper flakes
1 cup low-sodium chicken broth
½ teaspoon kosher salt
1 pound sea scallops, side muscle removed, if present, and patted very dry
kosher salt, to taste
freshly ground black pepper, to taste
1 large lemon, juiced
9-ounce package fresh fettuccine, cooked
½ bunch flat-leaf parsley leaves, finely chopped

In a large skillet, heat 1½ tablespoons butter and 1 tablespoon oil over medium heat and sauté asparagus for 3 - 4 minutes. Add peppers and sauté for 5 minutes. Add garlic and red pepper flakes; cook for 2 minutes. Stir in broth and ½ teaspoon salt; cook until vegetables are tender-crisp, lowering heat if broth begins to boil.

While vegetables finish cooking, begin cooking the scallops. In a separate large skillet over medium-high heat, melt the remaining 1 tablespoon butter with 1 tablespoon oil. Sprinkle scallops with salt and pepper and when the fat is hot, gently add scallops, taking care they do not touch. Do not move them until a brown crust has formed, about 2 - 3 minutes. Using tongs, carefully turn scallops over and continue to sear for several minutes or until the brown crust is apparent and they are opaque inside.

When the vegetables are ready, add lemon juice and toss with the freshly cooked pasta and parsley. Gently toss in the seared scallops.

# Crispy Chicken

*When the girls were in elementary school, I created a school cookbook as a fundraiser and submitted this as one of our family's favorites. This recipe was not only a family favorite of ours, but turned out to be a favorite by many who had bought the book and tried it. Although we always called it Crispy Chicken, the irony is that it isn't crispy at all!*

3 tablespoons unsalted butter, melted
1½ teaspoons Worcestershire
1 garlic clove, minced
1 teaspoon Dijon mustard
½ cup plain bread crumbs
½ cup freshly grated Parmesan-Reggiano
4 boneless, skinless chicken breast halves

Preheat oven to 325°. Combine butter, Worcestershire, garlic and Mustard in a pie plate. In a separate pie plate, combine bread crumbs and Parmesan.

Dip breasts one at a time, first in the butter mixture, then roll in the bread crumb mixture. Place in a 9" x 13" baking pan sprayed with cooking spray and bake for about 35 minutes.

# Baked "Fried" Chicken

2 large eggs
1 tablespoon Dijon mustard
1 cup plain Melba toast crumbs
1 teaspoon dried thyme leaves
¾ teaspoon kosher salt
½ teaspoon freshly ground black pepper
½ teaspoon dried oregano
2 tablespoons canola oil
4 - 6 boneless, skinless chicken breast halves

Preheat oven to 400°. Line a large rimmed baking sheet with aluminum foil and set a large rack over it. Spray cooking spray over rack and pan; set aside.

In a pie plate, beat eggs with mustard. In a separate pie plate, combine crumbs and seasonings. Taste and adjust seasoning. Using a fork, mix seasoned crumbs with oil.

Dip breasts, one at a time, first in the egg mixture, then press breasts into the seasoned crumbs. Set on the rack and bake for 20 - 25 minutes, depending on thickness of breasts.

Suggestion~
Use a food processor to make the crumbs. One 5-ounce package of Melba toast makes 1⅓ cups crumbs.

# Chicken Pizza

*This is actually Chicken Parmagiana, but when the girls were little, they were more inclined to eat it if I called it Chicken Pizza!*

1 egg
¾ cup Italian-seasoned bread crumbs
4 boneless, skinless chicken breast halves
½ cup canola oil
8-ounce can tomato purée
1 garlic clove, minced
¼ teaspoon dried basil
4 slices mozzarella
⅓ cup freshly grated Parmesan-Reggiano

Preheat oven to 325°. Beat egg in a pie plate. Place bread crumbs in a separate pie plate. Dip breasts one at a time, first in egg, then in bread crumbs; set aside.

Heat oil in a large skillet over medium-high heat. Add breasts and brown quickly on both sides. Place breasts on paper towels.

Discard remaining oil in the pan and wipe out with a paper towel. Add tomato purée, garlic and basil. Simmer over medium heat until thickened, about 10 minutes.

Transfer breasts to a 9" x 13" baking pan sprayed with cooking spray. Place one slice of mozzarella on top of each breast. Spread some sauce over mozzarella and sprinkle with Parmesan. Bake for 30 minutes.

# Honey Pistachio Chicken

*My sister, Lauren, shared this recipe, which combines both sweet and savory, creating a delectable flavor.*

1 egg
½ cup honey
½ cup finely chopped pistachios
½ cup plain bread crumbs
1 teaspoon dried oregano
½ teaspoon kosher salt
½ teaspoon freshly ground black pepper
4 boneless, skinless chicken breast halves
2 tablespoons unsalted butter, melted

Preheat oven to 375°. Whisk egg and honey together in a pie plate. Combine pistachios, bread crumbs, oregano, salt and pepper in a separate pie plate. Coat breasts, one at a time, first in the honey mixture, then press into the nut-crumb mixture.

Place breasts in a 9" x 13" baking pan sprayed with cooking spray; drizzle with butter. Bake for 30 minutes.

Suggestion~
The pistachios may be substituted with another type of nut, such as almond, macadamia or walnut.

# Lemon Garlic Chicken

½ cup plain bread crumbs
4 boneless, skinless chicken breast halves
¼ cup fresh lemon juice
¼ cup olive oil
2 tablespoons water
2 garlic cloves, minced
2 tablespoons chopped flat-leaf parsley leaves
½ teaspoon dried oregano
¼ teaspoon kosher salt
freshly ground black pepper, to taste

lemon wedges

Preheat oven to 325°. Place bread crumbs in a pie plate. Rinse chicken in cold water; shake off excess water. Roll damp breasts in bread crumbs and place in a 9" x 13" baking pan sprayed with cooking spray.

Combine remaining ingredients and spoon over the breasts. Bake for 35 minutes.

Serve with lemon wedges.

# Chicken Marbella

*This much-loved recipe is adapted from <u>The Silver Palate</u>.*

*Marinade:*
1 head garlic, peeled and minced
¼ cup dried oregano
¼ cup red wine vinegar
¼ cup olive oil
1 cup pitted dried plums, large dice
2 tablespoons capers + ½ teaspoon liquid from jar
4 bay leaves
kosher salt, to taste
freshly ground black pepper, to taste

6 boneless, skinless chicken breast halves
⅓ cup good-quality white wine
¼ cup light brown sugar

Place all marinade ingredients in a large zip-top bag; combine well. Add breasts and marinate overnight.

Preheat oven to 350°. Arrange contents of bag in a large baking pan, discarding bay leaves. Pour wine around the breasts and sprinkle with brown sugar. Bake for 30 minutes.

# Chicken in Phyllo Packets

*This is a lovely dish that would be perfect for a springtime dinner party.*

*Sauce:*
1½ cups mayonnaise
1 cup chopped scallions
⅓ cup fresh lemon juice
2 garlic cloves, minced
2 teaspoons dried tarragon

*Chicken:*
12 boneless, skinless chicken breast halves
kosher salt
freshly ground black pepper
24 sheets phyllo (if frozen, thawed in refrigerator overnight)
1⅓ cups unsalted butter, melted
⅓ cup freshly grated Parmesan-Reggiano

Combine all sauce ingredients; set aside.

Preheat oven to 375°. Lightly season chicken with salt and pepper. Place a sheet of phyllo on a work surface. Using a new 2"-wide paintbrush (see Details, page 9), brush with melted butter. Quickly place a second sheet on top of first and also brush with melted butter.

Spread about 1½ tablespoons of sauce on each side of a breast. Place the breast, on an angle, in the corner of the phyllo sheet. Fold corner over breast, then fold sides over and roll up to form a packet. Repeat with remaining breasts and phyllo.

Brush packets with remaining butter and sprinkle with Parmesan. Place in two 10" x 15" baking pans and bake for about 25 minutes.

Suggestion~
Packets may be frozen and baked later; do not brush with butter or sprinkle with Parmesan. Place packets on a cookie sheet and freeze for 1½ hours. When frozen, warp well in plastic wrap, then aluminum foil. Place in zip-top freezer bag and store in the freezer. Thaw overnight in the refrigerator; brush with butter and sprinkle with Parmesan just before baking.

# Chicken and Artichoke Casserole

½ cup plain bread crumbs
1 teaspoon poultry seasoning
4 tablespoons unsalted butter
1 small sweet yellow onion, diced
1 pound mushrooms, sliced
½ cup all-purpose flour
14-ounce can low-sodium chicken broth
2 cups milk, heated
8 chicken tenderloins, cut bite-size
1 package frozen artichokes, thawed and sliced

12-ounce package medium egg noodles, cooked

Preheat oven to 350°. In a small bowl, combine bread crumbs and seasoning; set aside.

Melt butter in a skillet over medium heat and sauté onions. When onions are almost cooked through, add mushrooms and sauté until mushrooms are soft. Reduce heat to medium-low and add flour; cook 3 minutes, stirring constantly.

Increase heat to medium and slowly add broth and milk; cook until thickened, stirring frequently. Add chicken and artichokes. Pour into a greased casserole dish. Sprinkle seasoned bread crumbs over casserole. Bake for 40 minutes.

Serve over noodles.

Suggestion~
The top edge of the artichoke can be tough, so trim accordingly.

# Chicken Wellingtons
# with Madeira Sauce

*These are terrific for a dinner party; not only are they made ahead and frozen, they make an impressive presentation and they're delicious!*

*Mushroom Duxelle:*
1 tablespoon cornstarch
2 tablespoons dry sherry
1 tablespoon unsalted butter
2 tablespoons finely minced shallots
1 pound mushrooms, diced
kosher salt, to taste
freshly ground black pepper, to taste
1 tablespoon finely chopped chives
½ teaspoon white truffle oil

*Chicken:*
1 sheet Pepperidge Farm frozen puff pastry, thawed overnight in the
   refrigerator
6 4-ounce boneless, skinless chicken breast halves, mignon removed
1 egg, beaten

In a small bowl, combine cornstarch and sherry to make a slurry; set aside.

In a large skillet over medium heat, melt butter and sauté shallots 2 - 3 minutes. Add mushrooms and sauté over high heat until most of the liquid is evaporated. Lower heat and season with salt and pepper. Stir in the slurry gradually and cook until mixture is thickened and paste-like. Allow it to cool somewhat; add chives and truffle oil. Transfer to a large flat dish and refrigerate to chill.

On a lightly floured surface, roll out the pastry sheet to 10" x 15". Cut into six 5" x 5" squares and lay them on a lightly floured surface. Cut a ½" diameter vent hole in the center of each square.

Place one-sixth of the chilled mushroom duxelle over each vent hole and spread it into an oval diagonally across dough, the same size as a breast.

Place a breast, boned-side up, on top of the duxelle. Bring the corners to the center, turn over and press into a flattened egg shape. Decorate the top with excess pastry, if desired, taking care not to cover vent hole completely.

Brush with beaten egg; repeat with remaining breasts. Place breasts on a cookie sheet and freeze for 1½ hours. When frozen, wrap well in plastic wrap, then aluminum foil. Place in zip-top freezer bag and store in the freezer.

Preheat oven to 375°. Bake frozen Wellingtons on a parchment-lined rimmed baking sheet for about 1 hour. Serve with Madeira Sauce.

# Madeira Sauce

3 tablespoons butter
1½ tablespoons all-purpose flour
¾ cup low-sodium chicken broth
3 tablespoons Madeira
kosher salt

In a small saucepan, melt butter over medium-low heat. Add flour and whisk 3 minutes. Add remaining ingredients and cook until thickened, whisking continuously. Season to taste with salt.

# Chicken Curry

6 chicken tenderloins, cut bite-size
2½ teaspoons curry powder, divided
kosher salt, to taste
freshly ground black pepper, to taste
3 tablespoons canola oil, divided
1 medium sweet yellow onion, chopped
½ cup grated carrots
1 small Granny Smith apple, peeled and finely diced
4 garlic cloves, minced
1 tablespoon grated fresh ginger
14-ounce can low-sodium chicken broth
1 tablespoon cornstarch
1 cup frozen petite peas
¼ cup Greek yogurt
¼ cup chopped fresh cilantro

steamed white rice

Season chicken with 1 teaspoon curry, salt and pepper. In a large skillet, heat 1½ tablespoons oil over medium-high heat and cook chicken, stirring, until halfway cooked through. Transfer to a bowl and set aside.

Reduce heat to medium and add remaining 1½ tablespoons oil. Add onions, carrots and apples, cooking until softened. Add garlic, ginger and remaining 1½ teaspoons curry, stirring constantly for 2 minutes. Whisk broth and cornstarch together and add to skillet. Bring to a boil, then reduce heat to medium and stir until sauce thickens.

Reduce heat to medium-low and add partially-cooked chicken and peas. Cook about 5 minutes, or until chicken is warmed and cooked through. Remove from heat and stir in yogurt and cilantro. Add salt and pepper to taste.

Serve on a bed of steamed white rice.


Suggestion~
If more heat is desired, add cayenne to taste.

# Chicken Tetrazzini

5 tablespoons unsalted butter, divided
1 tablespoon olive oil
1 sweet yellow onion, chopped
1 pound mushrooms, sliced
kosher salt
freshly ground black pepper
3 garlic cloves, minced
¼ cup all-purpose flour
2½ cups hot milk
1 teaspoon kosher salt
¼ teaspoon cayenne
3 tablespoons dry sherry
½ cup freshly grated Parmesan-Reggiano + more for topping
8 chicken tenderloins, cut bite-size
1 cup frozen petite peas, thawed
8 ounces thin spaghetti, broken in half and cooked

In a large skillet, melt 1 tablespoon butter with oil over medium heat and sauté onions until almost softened. Add mushrooms and, when partially cooked, season to taste with salt and pepper. When mushrooms are almost cooked through, add garlic and cook for 2 minutes. Use a slotted spoon to transfer vegetables to a large bowl; set aside. Discard any liquid in the pan.

Preheat oven to 350°. Reduce heat to medium-low and, using the same pan (leave unwashed), melt remaining 4 tablespoons butter. Add flour and cook 3 minutes, whisking constantly. Slowly add milk and increase heat to medium, whisking constantly until thickened. If sauce begins to bubble, reduce heat. Whisk in salt, cayenne and sherry. Remove from heat and whisk in Parmesan.

Add the chicken and peas to the onions and mushrooms. Mix in spaghetti. Pour the white sauce over all and combine well.

Transfer mixture to a 2.5-quart casserole dish sprayed with cooking spray. Grate Parmesan generously over top. Bake for 45 minutes.

# Chicken Veggie Stir-fry

*Laura shared this tasty recipe. The little squeeze of lime has a big impact!*

9 ounces ramen noodles
4 tablespoons peanut or canola oil, divided
⅓ cup low-sodium soy sauce
¼ cup packed light brown sugar
¼ cup unseasoned rice vinegar (preferably Marukan)
¼ cup Asian sweet red chili sauce
1½ teaspoons sesame oil
6 chicken tenderloins, cut bite-size
1 tablespoon cornstarch
1 small red onion, cut large chop
4 garlic cloves, minced
2 tablespoons grated fresh ginger
8 ounces sugar snap peas, halved
1 red bell pepper, large chop
1 orange pepper, large chop
2 medium zucchini, large chop

lime wedges

Cook noodles per directions on package. Drain and toss with 1 tablespoon oil; set aside.

Whisk soy sauce, sugar, vinegar, chili sauce and sesame oil together in a small bowl. Place chicken pieces in a separate small bowl and toss with ¼ cup of the soy sauce mixture, then the cornstarch. Set both bowls aside.

Heat a wok or large skillet with 2 tablespoons oil over medium-high heat. When oil is hot, add the chicken and stir for several minutes or until chicken is almost cooked through. Transfer chicken back to the bowl.

Heat remaining 1 tablespoon oil in the pan, add onions and stir for 2 minutes. Add the garlic and ginger and stir for 1 minute. Add the remaining vegetables and stir for 2 minutes. Add about ½ of the sauce and continue stirring until the vegetables are crisp-tender.

Add the noodles and chicken, tossing to combine with the vegetables. Add remaining sauce and stir-fry for another minute or so until everything is coated with the sauce.

Serve with lime wedges.

Suggestion~
Stir-frying is a very fast cooking method, so it is essential to have everything prepped and within reach before the cooking begins. Once the first item of food is in the pan, stir continuously until everything is cooked.

# Apricot Chicken

*When you don't have time to prep and need to throw something together quickly, this is a great go-to!*

4 boneless, skinless chicken breast halves
½ cup apricot preserves or jam
1 tablespoon low-sodium soy sauce

Preheat oven to 325°. Place breasts in a 9″ x 13″ baking pan sprayed with cooking spray. Place preserves in a small bowl and combine well with soy sauce. Spoon half the sauce on top of breasts and bake for 35 minutes. Spoon remaining sauce over breasts before serving.

# Chicken Quesadillas

*Picking up a roasted chicken at the market makes this especially easy.
Barry likes hot salsa and I prefer a medium-spicy one, so with this dish,
we're both happy!*

1 ear white corn, kernels cut off
1 large jalapeno, minced
8 ounces cherry or grape tomatoes, halved
1 red, orange or yellow pepper, chopped
½ small red onion, diced
2 cooked chicken breast halves, shredded
½ cup grated Cheddar or Jack cheese
15-ounce can black beans, rinsed and drained
medium-size flour tortillas
salsa of your choice

sliced avocado
lime wedges

Preheat oven to 400°. In a large bowl, combine all ingredients, except
tortillas and salsa.

Line a large rimmed baking sheet with aluminum foil and spray lightly with
cooking spray. Place 2 tortillas on the foil. Spoon some of the chicken
mixture on each tortilla and top with salsa. (If you have extra filling, make
more quesadillas or refrigerate the mixture for a day or two.) Place another
tortilla over each of the fillings and cover the pan with aluminum foil. Bake
for 20 minutes.

Serve topped with avocado and lime on the side.


Suggestion~
If using different salsas, tear the end of the foil a bit near the hot one to tell
them apart.

# Grilled Chicken with Mango Avocado Salsa

*This salsa has great summer flavors. It doesn't have to be part of an entrée; just make a double or triple batch and bring out the tortilla chips!*

*Chicken:*
2 tablespoons fresh lime juice
½ cup olive oil
3 - 4 boneless, skinless chicken breast halves
kosher salt, to taste
freshly ground pepper, to taste

*Salsa:*
1 ripe mango, chopped
½ red pepper, small dice
1 small jalapeno, minced
3 tablespoons minced red onion
1 tablespoon minced cilantro leaves
1 lime, juiced
generous pinch kosher salt
small avocado, chopped

Place lime juice, oil, breasts, salt and pepper in a zip-top bag. Refrigerate for several hours to marinate.

Combine all salsa ingredients, except avocado. Cover and refrigerate 1 - 2 hours.

Remove salsa from the refrigerator about 20 minutes before serving and gently stir in avocado. When ready to cook the chicken, discard the marinade; grill. Top the grilled breasts with the salsa.


Suggestion~
The salsa also complements meaty fish, such as salmon and swordfish.

# Turkey Balls

*I grew up in the Midwest and this recipe has its roots there. The sauce was originally made for ground beef meatballs, but I prefer using ground turkey as it produces a lighter meatball. I always serve this with steamed red potatoes. The sauce is just made for it!*

12-ounce jar chili sauce (preferably Heinz)
½ 18-ounce jar grape jelly (preferably Welch's)
1 tablespoon dried minced onion, divided
2 large eggs
¼ cup milk
¼ teaspoon kosher salt
¼ teaspoon freshly ground black pepper
3 slices buttermilk, potato or other 'light' bread
1½ pounds lean ground turkey

In a large stock pot, heat chili sauce, jelly and 2 teaspoons minced onion over medium-low heat until jelly melts. Reduce heat to low.

In a large bowl, beat eggs with milk, remaining 1 teaspoon minced onion, salt and pepper. Tear up bread into small pieces and soak in egg mixture about 5 minutes.

Add ground turkey to bread mixture and, using your hands, gently mix until just combined. Form into 6 balls.

Transfer balls to pot, spooning some sauce over the top and sides of each ball. Cook for 20 minutes. Gently turn balls over and again spoon some sauce over them. Cook for an additional 20 minutes.

# Roasted Vegetable Turkey Chili

14-ounce can low-sodium chicken broth
2 bay leaves
1 teaspoon cumin
1 red onion, ¼" slices
2 red peppers, halved and seeded
3 jalapenos, halved and seeded
1¼ pounds lean ground turkey
15-ounce can chopped tomatoes, with liquid
28-ounce can crushed tomatoes with purée
¼ cup water
1 teaspoon cider vinegar
2 teaspoons kosher salt
1½ teaspoons chili powder
1 tablespoon minced garlic
15-ounce can black beans, rinsed and drained
½ 16-ounce bag frozen petite white corn, thawed
¾ cup elbow macaroni

Place broth, bay leaves and cumin in a large stock pot; bring to a simmer.

Preheat oven to Broil. Line a large rimmed baking sheet with aluminum foil. Place onions, peppers and jalapenos on foil; peppers and jalapenos skin-side up. Broil until onion slices are browned and the pepper and jalapeno skins are blackened. Transfer vegetables to a cutting board.

Place turkey on the foil and shape into a rectangle, flattening to about 1½ ". Broil until well browned on one side. When peppers and jalapenos are cool enough to handle, peel and discard the skins. Chop all the vegetables and add to stock pot. Break up the turkey into very small pieces and add to the pot; simmer 10 minutes.

Stir in tomatoes, water, vinegar, salt and chili powder. Cover and simmer 20 minutes. Add garlic, beans and corn, macaroni; simmer, uncovered, 15 - 20 minutes, or until macaroni is tender. Remove bay leaves before serving.


Suggestion~
When serving, offer any of the following accompaniments:
diced avocado            diced red onion
sour cream               chopped cilantro leaves
crushed tortilla chips   grated Cheddar or Jack cheese

# Turkey Vegetable Cobbler

*This is a great way to use leftover turkey from Thanksgiving. To quote my younger daughter directly from the recipe where she wrote this many years ago: "I love this! Julia's favorite winter dinner!!! Thank you, Mommy! xoxoxo" That says it all!*

*Cobbler:*
1 pound carrots, sliced and cooked
½ 10-ounce bag frozen pearl onions, thawed and halved
1¼ cups frozen petite peas, thawed
4 cups large-chunk cooked turkey breast
½ cup unsalted butter, divided
2 medium leeks, white part only, finely chopped
1 pound mushrooms, large dice
7 tablespoons all-purpose flour
14-ounce can low-sodium chicken broth
1 cup milk, heated
¼ teaspoon kosher salt
¼ teaspoon white pepper
2 tablespoons finely chopped flat-leaf parsley leaves
2 teaspoons dried thyme leaves
poultry seasoning, to taste

*Cobbler dough:*
1¾ cups all-purpose flour
1 tablespoon baking powder
½ teaspoon kosher salt
¼ cup freshly grated Parmesan-Reggiano + extra for sprinkling
6 tablespoons unsalted butter, diced and frozen for 20 minutes
½ cup milk

1 egg, beaten

Place the carrots, onions, peas and turkey in a large bowl; set aside.

In a large saucepan, melt 2 tablespoons butter over medium heat and sauté leeks for about 3 minutes. Add the mushrooms and sauté about 5 minutes. Place them in the bowl with the vegetables and turkey; set aside. Wipe out pan with a paper towel.

Using the same pan, melt remaining 6 tablespoons butter over medium heat.

Add flour and cook, whisking constantly, for 3 minutes. Slowly add the broth and milk, whisking until thickened and smooth. Add remaining ingredients. Taste and adjust seasonings. Pour the white sauce over the vegetables and turkey, stirring to combine.

Grease a 9" x 13" baking pan and transfer cobbler mixture to pan.

Preheat oven to 400°. For cobbler dough, place the dry ingredients and ¼ cup Parmesan in a food processor. Blend for 1 minute. Add butter and pulse until all flour is incorporated. Add milk through the feed tube and process just until a ball is formed.

On a floured surface, roll out dough to fit the pan, then place it on top of the cobbler mixture.

Brush dough with beaten egg and sprinkle with Parmesan. Place the pan on a large rimmed baking sheet. Bake for 30 - 35 minutes, or until crust is browned. Let stand 10 minutes before serving.


Suggestion~
The turkey may be substituted with cooked and shredded chicken.

# Veggie Turkey Burgers

*This is not your typical plain turkey burger; the vegetables and Parmesan add so much flavor.*

2 tablespoons olive oil
1 small sweet yellow onion, chopped
1 red pepper, chopped
kosher salt, to taste
freshly ground black pepper, to taste
8 ounces mushrooms, roughly chopped
1 garlic clove, minced
¼ cup Italian-seasoned bread crumbs
¼ cup freshly grated Parmesan-Reggiano
1 egg
1½ pounds lean ground turkey

Heat oil in a skillet over medium heat and sauté onions and red peppers a few minutes; season well with salt and pepper.

Cover pan and reduce heat to medium-low; cook about 7 - 8 minutes, stirring halfway. Add mushrooms and continue cooking, covered, for another 5 minutes, until vegetables are tender, stirring halfway; season well with salt and pepper. Stir in garlic and cook, uncovered, for 2 minutes.

Transfer vegetables to a large bowl and cool them quickly by placing the bowl in the freezer for 20 minutes (no longer), stirring occasionally.

Add bread crumbs and Parmesan to the vegetables. Make a well and beat the egg; stir into the vegetable mixture. Add turkey and, using your hands, gently mix until just combined. Form the mixture into 6 patties, cover with plastic wrap and refrigerate for several hours; grill.

# Marinated Flank Steak

*Marinade:*
1 garlic clove
¼ cup canola oil
2 tablespoons fresh lemon juice
2 tablespoons low-sodium soy sauce
2 tablespoons honey
1 tablespoon cider vinegar
1½ teaspoons dried minced onion
¾ teaspoon kosher salt
½ teaspoon sugar
½ teaspoon freshly ground black pepper
¼ teaspoon dry mustard
¼ teaspoon dried rosemary
⅛ teaspoon powdered ginger

1½-pound flank steak

With food processor running, drop garlic through feed tube and mince. Add remaining marinade ingredients and process until smooth.

Place the flank steak in a zip-top bag. Pour marinade over both sides and refrigerate at least 8 hours.

Remove from refrigerator 1 hour before cooking. Discard marinade and grill or broil steak. Let steak rest 5 minutes before slicing. Hold the knife on a 45° angle and cut into thin slices.

# Marinated Beef Tenderloin

*My son-in-law, Dave, served this on a 4th of July in Milwaukee. Although the fireworks from Summerfest just across the street were phenomenal, they almost paled in comparison to this flavor!*

*Marinade:*
<1 cup packed brown sugar
½ cup Worcestershire
¼ cup + 2 tablespoons brandy
¼ cup low-sodium soy sauce
2 tablespoons chopped garlic
1 tablespoon kosher salt
1 tablespoon freshly ground black pepper

1 whole beef tenderloin or 4 - 5 filets

Combine marinade ingredients in a zip-top bag. Add the meat and marinate overnight for whole tenderloin or all day for filets.

Remove meat from the refrigerator 1 hour before cooking. While grill is heating, drain marinade into a small skillet and boil marinade gently until reduced and thickened; let cool a bit.

Grill meat and allow it to rest before slicing: 10 minutes for whole tenderloin or 5 minutes for filets. Spoon some of the reduction over the meat when serving. Transfer remaining reduction to a gravy boat for passing.

# Spice Rub for Steak

*My brother, Mitchell, was right; this rub adds incredible flavor to a simple steak. When he emailed the recipe, he simply said, "Your meat with this."*

1 tablespoon each: kosher salt, chili powder, finely ground dark roast
   coffee beans, dark brown sugar
2 teaspoons: freshly ground black pepper
1 teaspoon each: unsweetened cocoa powder, garlic powder
½ teaspoon each: ground ginger, ground cinnamon
¼ teaspoon: cumin

olive oil
steaks of your choice

Combine the seasonings in a small bowl; set aside.

Remove steaks from the refrigerator 1 hour before cooking. Pat steaks dry, brush all over with oil and coat the meat with the rub. Grill steaks; let meat rest 5 minutes before serving.


# Balsamic Glaze

*This syrupy glaze is both tangy and sweet. Drizzle it on grilled steak, chicken or fish. It also works well with vegetables, particularly when grilled or roasted, or with fruit, such as strawberries and peaches.*

1 cup good-quality balsamic vinegar

In a small saucepan, bring vinegar to a boil, then reduce heat and hold at a gentle simmer. Simmer for about 30 minutes, checking it periodically and reducing the heat as needed to maintain a gentle simmer. The glaze is ready when the vinegar reduces by about half and is syrupy. Cool completely, then store in an airtight container in the refrigerator.


Suggestion~
After the vinegar has simmered about 15 minutes, season it with freshly ground black pepper, to taste, and/or the juice of half an orange, or to taste.

# Hot Sides

~

# Steamed Brussels Sprouts

*Although this is such a basic recipe, I decided to include it because some find Brussels sprouts to be bitter and it's possible that the cooking method may contribute to that. If that's been your experience, you might want to give this a try.*

1 pound Brussels sprouts, trimmed
½ cup water
½ teaspoon kosher salt
1 tablespoon unsalted butter, room temperature
kosher salt
freshly ground black pepper

In a 2-quart saucepan, bring whole sprouts, water and salt to a boil over medium-high heat.

Lower heat, cover and simmer, stirring occasionally, until a knife tip goes easily into the stem end, about 8 - 10 minutes.

Drain and stir in butter until melted. Season to taste with salt and pepper.

# Shredded Brussels Sprouts

1 tablespoon unsalted butter
1 tablespoon olive oil
1 small sweet yellow onion, chopped
2 garlic cloves, minced
12 ounces mushrooms, sliced
1 pound Brussels sprouts, trimmed and shredded
grated zest of 1 lemon
1½ tablespoons fresh lemon juice
kosher salt
freshly ground black pepper
2 - 3 tablespoons freshly grated Parmesan-Reggiano

In a large skillet, melt butter with oil over medium-high heat and sauté onion for 5 minutes. Add garlic and mushrooms, cook 1 minute.

Reduce heat to medium, add sprouts and cook for a few minutes, stirring frequently. Cover and continue cooking until tender, stirring periodically, about 15 minutes.

Add lemon zest and juice. Season to taste with salt and pepper.

Remove from heat and add Parmesan, to taste.


Suggestion~
A quick way to shred the sprouts is to fill the feed tube of a food processor with whole sprouts and use the slicing blade to shred.

# Roasted Brussels Sprouts with Mushrooms and Chestnuts

*Delivering a wonderful combination of flavors, this is a rich and satisfying side dish to offer as part of a special autumn or winter dinner.*

1 pound Brussels sprouts, trimmed and halved through stem
1½ tablespoons olive oil
kosher salt
freshly ground black pepper
8 ounces sliced mushrooms
2 tablespoons sherry vinegar, divided
2 tablespoons unsalted butter, room temperature
2 garlic cloves, minced
¼ teaspoon dried red pepper flakes, or to taste
1 teaspoon honey
4 ounces jarred roasted chestnuts, large chop
1 tablespoon water

Preheat oven to 425°. Place sprouts on a rimmed baking sheet and toss with enough olive oil to lightly coat; season to taste with salt and pepper. Lay evenly in the pan, cut side down, and roast for about 25 minutes, or until cut sides are brown.

When sprouts are almost done, heat 1½ tablespoons olive oil in a large skillet over medium-high heat until smoking. Add mushrooms and cook, without stirring, for 1 minute. Shake pan and continue to brown for 2 more minutes; season with salt and pepper. Stir in 1 tablespoon vinegar.

Add butter, garlic, pepper flakes and roasted sprouts; cook until butter is browned, about 1 minute. Stir in the honey and chestnuts. Season to taste with salt and pepper. Add remaining 1 tablespoon vinegar and water; stir to combine.

# Orange~Glazed Carrots

6 carrots, cut into ¼" slices diagonally
finely grated zest of 1 orange
½ cup fresh orange juice
¼ cup dry sherry
1 teaspoon packed light brown sugar
2 teaspoons cornstarch
1 teaspoon grated fresh ginger
1 tablespoon unsalted butter

Steam carrots until just tender; drain.

While carrots cook, combine remaining ingredients, except butter, in a small saucepan. Cook over medium heat, stirring until thickened.

Lower heat and add butter, stirring until it melts. Add hot carrots and toss to coat.

# Candy Carrots

*Even kids who don't like vegetables just can't resist Candy Carrots… the name alone will bring them to the table!*

1 pound carrots, sliced
2 tablespoons unsalted butter
2 - 3 tablespoons packed light brown sugar

Steam carrots until tender.

When carrots are almost cooked through, melt butter in a medium saucepan over medium-low heat. Add brown sugar, stirring to dissolve. Drain cooked carrots and immediately toss in the butter-sugar mixture until coated.

# Corn Custard

*The simplicity of this dish is deceiving because it tastes so decadent. We have my brother, Mitchell, to thank for it. However, be forewarned, you might want to wear an apron when grating the corn... it gets messy!*

6 ears white corn
1 tablespoon unsalted butter
½ teaspoon kosher salt
<¼ teaspoon cayenne

lime wedges

Preheat oven to 350°. Place a box grater in a 10" cast iron skillet. Using the large holes, grate corn into the skillet. When cob has been completely grated, scrape it against the skillet's edge to extract even more corn and milk. Spread corn and milk evenly in the pan and bake for about 25 minutes, or until it looks puffed and surface is mostly dry.

Adjust heat to Broil and move skillet to top rack. Broil for a few minutes until the top lightly browns. Remove from oven and stir in butter, salt and cayenne. Taste and adjust seasoning.

Serve with lime wedges.


Suggestion~
The cayenne and lime are not strictly necessary (but are oh, so delicious!), so omit them for a more pristine corn taste.

# Sautéed Corn and Peppers

2 tablespoons canola oil
1 sweet yellow onion, chopped
1 red bell pepper, chopped
1 orange bell pepper, chopped
kosher salt, to taste
freshly ground black pepper, to taste
2 jalapenos, finely diced
4 ears white corn, kernels cut off
2 tablespoons unsalted butter

Heat oil in a skillet over medium heat and sauté onions and peppers until almost soft; season with salt and pepper. Reduce heat to medium-low and add jalapeno; cook a few minutes.

Add corn and cook about 4 minutes, or until corn is hot but still crisp. Add butter and stir until melted. Taste and adjust seasoning.


# Roasted Mushrooms

1 pound shiitake, white or crimini mushrooms, sliced
1 red or sweet yellow onion, thinly sliced
2 tablespoons unsalted butter, melted
1 tablespoon white truffle oil
½ teaspoon dried thyme leaves
kosher salt
freshly ground black pepper

Preheat oven to 400°. Toss all ingredients, except salt and pepper, on a large rimmed baking sheet; arrange in an even layer. Season to taste with salt and pepper.

Roast for 30 - 35 minutes.

# Mellow Mushrooms

*Rich in flavor and dark in color, these mushrooms pair well with a simple roasted or grilled meat.*

¼ cup unsalted butter
1 large sweet yellow onion, large chop
½ cup packed light brown sugar
2 tablespoons Dijon mustard
2 tablespoons Worcestershire
¾ cup good-quality dry red wine
½ teaspoon kosher salt
½ teaspoon freshly ground black pepper
2 pounds large white mushrooms, thickly sliced

In a large skillet, melt butter over medium-high heat and sauté onions until partially softened. While onions cook, combine sugar, mustard and Worcestershire in a small bowl, stirring until smooth. Blend in wine, salt and pepper; set aside.

Add mushrooms to the skillet and cook until they are partially softened. Stir in the wine mixture and reduce the heat to an active simmer. Simmer, stirring periodically, for about 45 - 55 minutes to allow the sauce to reduce and absorb into the mushrooms. Taste and adjust seasoning.

# Cipollini Onions with Orange Balsamic Glaze

*Always a lover of onions, Barry fell in love with cipollinis while visiting Julia in Florence. This recipe brings back some of the flavors of that remarkable trip.*

2 - 3 pounds cipollini onions, untrimmed
2 tablespoons unsalted butter
2 tablespoons olive oil
3 ounces fresh orange juice
3 ounces balsamic vinegar
1 tablespoon water
kosher salt, to taste
freshly ground black pepper, to taste

Bring a large saucepan of water to boil. Add onions and cook 2 minutes; drain and cool. Peel onions and cut off root ends.

In a large skillet, melt butter with oil over medium heat. Add onions and sauté until brown and tender, about 10 minutes.

Add remaining ingredients. Reduce heat to medium-low and simmer until liquid reduces and thickens a bit, about 15 - 20 minutes.

# Parmesan Gremolata

*A classic Italian condiment, gremolata adds a burst of flavor to cooked vegetables. It traditionally does not have Parmesan as an ingredient, but adding it makes it even more flavorful.*

3 tablespoons minced flat-leaf parsley
3 tablespoons freshly grated Parmesan-Reggiano
2 small garlic cloves, minced
grated zest of 2 large lemons

1 - 1½ pounds vegetables of choice, such as asparagus, broccoli, Brussels sprouts, green beans or zucchini

Combine parsley, Parmesan, garlic and lemon zest in a bowl; set aside.

Steam or roast vegetables and immediately toss with the gremolata.

Suggestion~
Add 2 tablespoons toasted and finely chopped almonds, pine nuts or pecans.

Add other fresh herbs, such as thyme or tarragon.

The lemon zest may be substituted with orange zest.

# Roasted Vegetable Medley

*Pretty colors coupled with the balsamic's sweet and sour flavor make this side dish deliciously attractive.*

2 red onions, large chop
1 pound carrots, sliced ¼" diagonally
3 red, yellow or orange bell peppers, cut into 1" squares
olive oil
kosher salt
freshly ground black pepper
3 tablespoons balsamic vinegar, or more to taste

Preheat oven to 425°. Place vegetables on large rimmed baking sheet and toss with oil to lightly coat. Season to taste with salt and pepper; toss again.

Roast for about 35 - 45 minutes or until the vegetables are al dente, stirring occasionally. Taste and adjust seasoning. Stir in vinegar and cook an additional 10 - 15 minutes.

# Basic Roasted Vegetables from A-Z

*Roasting vegetables caramelizes them and brings out their natural sugar. Cauliflower is truly transformed! Most veggies roast beautifully and are super easy to do. When cutting the vegetables, keep in mind that they'll all shrink a bit, with the softer ones shrinking more.*

*Vegetable prep:*
asparagus – snap off tough ends; line up in pan
bell peppers (red/orange/yellow) – cut into 1" squares or ½" wide strips
broccoli – using a vegetable peeler, peel tough outer layers; cut lengthwise
  into halves or quarters, keeping stalks uniform in size
Brussels sprouts – trim ends, remove outer leaves and cut in half through
  stem; arrange cut-side down
butternut squash – peel, cut in half and scoop out seeds, cut into cubes
carrots – cut baby carrots in half or keep whole, or cut ¼" slices from whole
  carrots
cauliflower – cut into medium-size florets
corn – cut kernels off cob
eggplant – cut into 1" cubes
fennel – cut stalks from bulb, cut into wedges through core; arrange
  cut-side down and turn over halfway through
green beans – trim ends
leeks – cut in half vertically, rinse interior without disassembling, drain well
  and drizzle with oil; cut 1" pieces and arrange cut-side down
mushrooms – button, keep whole; crimini, cut in half; portobellos, scrape
  gills and cut ½" slices
onions (yellow/red) – cut 1" pieces or ½" slices
red potatoes – cut into large chunks and place cut-side down
zucchini – trim ends and quarter lengthwise; place cut-side down and turn
  over halfway through

olive oil – regular or flavored
kosher salt
freshly ground black pepper

Place a large rimmed baking sheet in the oven and preheat to 425°. Place vegetables of choice in a large bowl and drizzle with oil, taking care that there is just enough oil to lightly coat them. When the oven reaches temperature, remove the pan and quickly arrange vegetables in a single layer.

Roasting times will vary based on the density and size of the vegetable; most need at least 15 minutes and some up to 40. Zucchini probably cooks the fastest while Brussels sprouts, cauliflower and potatoes take the longest. With the exception of Brussels sprouts, fennel, leeks and zucchini, stir vegetables periodically during the roasting process. When vegetables are done, taste and adjust seasoning.

Suggestion~
Lemon olive oil is delicious on asparagus, broccoli, Brussels sprouts, eggplant and zucchini. Feel free to experiment with different flavored oils.

Adding a dash of lemon juice and fresh herbs after cooking also adds zip.

# Orzo

2 tablespoons unsalted butter
1 cup orzo
2¼ cups low-sodium chicken broth, boiling
½ teaspoon kosher salt

Over medium heat, melt butter in a 2-quart saucepan and stir in orzo. Cook 3 minutes; add boiling broth and salt.

Reduce heat to low, cover and cook 20 minutes.

Suggestion~
Add any of the following once the orzo is cooked:
freshly grated Parmesan
crumbled Feta
frozen petite peas, thawed
toasted pine nuts

# Our Favorite Rice
## aka Rice Pilaf

*My sister, Lauren, received this recipe from her college boyfriend's mom. It's a recipe we used when we had our little catering business, "My Sister and I." In our family, it became known as "our favorite rice."*

4 tablespoons unsalted butter
¼ cup fideo or thin spaghetti, broken into small pieces
1 cup long-grain white rice
2 cups low-sodium chicken broth, boiling
1 teaspoon kosher salt

Melt butter in a 2-quart saucepan over medium-low heat. Add fideo or spaghetti and stir until browned. Add rice, stirring to coat the grains with butter.

Add broth and salt, stir and cover pan. Reduce heat to low and cook for 25 minutes.

Remove from the heat and fluff with a fork. Recover the pan and let it stand off heat for 20 minutes.


Suggestion~
When the rice is removed from the heat, use a fork to gently stir in any of the following:
toasted pine nuts
frozen petite peas, thawed
dried apricots, julienned

# Barley and Pine Nut Pilaf

*This hearty dish, when paired with meat and roasted vegetables, makes a classic winter dinner.*

6 tablespoons unsalted butter
⅓ cup pine nuts
1 cup pearled barley, rinsed and drained
1 cup thinly sliced scallions
½ cup chopped flat-leaf parsley leaves
2 14-ounce cans low-sodium chicken broth, boiling
1 teaspoon kosher salt

Preheat oven to 350°. Melt butter in a skillet over medium heat and brown pine nuts. Remove with a slotted spoon and place in a 2-quart casserole dish.

In the same pan, sauté barley and onions until barley is lightly toasted. Add the barley mixture, along with the parsley, to the casserole dish.

Pour boiling broth over all. Add salt and stir to blend.

Bake, uncovered, for 1 hour and 10 minutes. Stir well before serving.

# Apple Kugel

*There's no doubt that our family loves kugel. Julia loved it so much
when she was little, that she named one of her stuffed puppies Kugel!*

8 ounces cream cheese, room temperature
½ cup unsalted butter, room temperature
½ cup sugar
1 teaspoon ground cinnamon
4 large eggs
¾ cup milk
1 teaspoon pure vanilla extract
2 Granny Smith apples, peeled and cut into small chunks
8 ounces medium egg noodles, cooked, rinsed and drained

Preheat oven to 350°. In the bowl of a stand mixer, beat the cream cheese
and butter until just combined. Beat in sugar and cinnamon; add eggs, milk
and vanilla. Stir in apples and noodles.

Pour into a greased and lightly floured 7" x 11" baking pan; bake for
1 hour.

Let cool 10 minutes, cut into squares and serve.


Suggestion~
Add ½ cup golden raisins.

# Baked Potato Wedges

¼ cup ketchup
3 tablespoons unsalted butter, melted
1 tablespoon packed dark brown sugar
¼ teaspoon kosher salt
¼ teaspoon freshly ground black pepper
2 large russet potatoes

Preheat oven to 400°. In a small bowl, combine all ingredients, except potatoes; set aside.

Cut each potato in half lengthwise, then cut each half lengthwise into 4 wedges. Make about 6 - 8 deep angle cuts in each wedge, taking care not to cut through the skin.

Spray an aluminum foil-covered baking sheet with cooking spray. Place wedges on foil, skin-side down. Using the back of a spoon, smear enough of the ketchup mixture on cut surfaces to lightly coat.

Bake for about 50 - 60 minutes, or until potatoes are fork-tender.


# Garlic~Roasted Potatoes

red potatoes, skin on and cut into large bite-size pieces
1 garlic clove for each pound of potatoes, minced
olive oil
dried thyme or rosemary leaves, to taste
kosher salt, to taste
freshly ground black pepper, to taste

Preheat oven to 400°. Place potatoes and garlic on large rimmed baking sheet and add enough oil to lightly coat potatoes; toss with herbs and seasoning. Arrange evenly in pan and roast for 45 - 60 minutes, stirring occasionally. Roast potatoes until the outsides are crispy and the insides are tender.

# Twice~Baked Potatoes

3 russet potatoes
canola oil
2 large heads garlic
olive oil
¼ cup low-sodium chicken broth
½ cup sour cream
½ cup freshly grated Parmesan-Reggiano
2 scallions, thinly sliced
¾ teaspoon kosher salt
freshly ground black pepper, to taste

Preheat oven to 425°. Rub the potato skins with canola oil and, using a fork, pierce potatoes all over; place potatoes on a baking sheet.

Remove outer layer of paper from each head of garlic. Slice off the top quarter or so of each head and discard. Keep the cloves attached to the stem and drizzle the exposed cloves with a bit of olive oil. Wrap the garlic heads in aluminum foil.

Place the garlic packet on the baking sheet with the potatoes and bake for at least 1 hour, or until potatoes and inner cloves of garlic are very soft when tested with a knife. Let stand until they are cool enough to handle.

Reduce the oven temperature to 350°. Press the garlic heads from the bottom and sides to release the roasted cloves and place in a bowl. Halve the potatoes and carefully scoop out the pulp, leaving a ¼" shell. (Use a small melon baller to make scooping out the potato almost effortless.) Place the potato pulp in the bowl with the garlic. Add the broth and, using a potato masher, mash the potatoes and garlic together. Add the remaining ingredients and mix well. Taste and adjust seasoning.

Pile potato mixture into potato shells. Bake for 30 - 40 minutes.

Suggestion~
If you prefer to have the shells heaping with filling, pile the mixture into 4 or 5 of the shells, rather than using all 6.

Twice-baked potatoes may be made a day in advance and refrigerated; just increase baking time.

# Make~Ahead Potato Pancakes

*Given the mess that frying potato pancakes can create, it's helpful that they may be made ahead and reheated in the oven.*

1½ pounds white potatoes, grated
1 tablespoon grated yellow onion
1 egg, beaten
½ cup all-purpose flour
¼ teaspoon kosher salt
canola oil

Place grated potatoes in a towel-lined colander for 10 minutes. Squeeze out moisture and combine with remaining ingredients, except oil.

Heat 3 tablespoons oil in a large skillet over high heat. Using a ¼-cup dry measure for each pancake, fry until browned on bottom. Turn pancakes over and brown other side. (Take care not to fry them too crispy, as they will crisp up later when baked.) Cook in batches, wiping out the pan with a paper towel.

Cool on paper towels; gently press the top of pancakes with paper towels to absorb excess oil. When completely cool, place in a single layer on a cookie sheet and freeze for 45 minutes. Store in a freezer zip-top bag.

When ready to reheat, preheat oven to 375°. Place frozen pancakes in a single layer on an aluminum foil-lined baking sheet; bake for 20 minutes, turning halfway.


Suggestion~
Serve the pancakes with Applesauce (page 150).

# Garlic Mashed Potatoes

1½ pounds red or Yukon Gold potatoes, skin on and cut into chunks
kosher salt
1 cup milk + more, if needed
¼ cup unsalted butter
1 head garlic, cloves peeled
½ cup sour cream
kosher salt, to taste
3 scallions, thinly sliced

Place potatoes in a saucepan and fill with cold water and enough salt to be well-salted, taking care that water covers potatoes. Bring water to a boil over medium heat and cook until potatoes are tender.

While potatoes are cooking, simmer milk, butter and garlic in a small saucepan until garlic is tender; set aside.

Drain potatoes and place them back in the pan over medium-low heat, shaking pan to dry and distribute potatoes. Pour garlic milk over potatoes and gently mash. Add sour cream and salt. Thin with more milk, if desired. Fold in scallions.

# Sweet Potatoes Amaretto

*Another sweet potato option, driven with flavors of orange and apricot, is 'Apricot Sweet Potatoes.' The recipe may be found in the Thanksgiving chapter.*

5 pounds orange-flesh sweet potatoes
¼ cup unsalted butter, room temperature
¼ - ½ cup light brown sugar
¼ cup Amaretto, or more to taste
¼ cup orange marmalade
2 teaspoons ground ginger
24 (12 packages) Lazzaroni Amaretti di Saronno cookies
½ cup unsalted butter, chilled and cut in chunks

Preheat oven to 400°. Prick potatoes all over with a fork and place them on an aluminum foil-lined large rimmed baking sheet. Roast for about 1 hour, or until they are soft. Set them aside until cool enough to handle.

Reduce oven temperature to 350°. Split potatoes open and scoop the flesh into a large bowl; mash. Add remaining ingredients, except cookies and ½ cup butter, in the order given. Transfer to a greased baking dish.

Pulverize cookies in the work bowl of a food processor. Add the ½ cup butter and pulse until incorporated.

Sprinkle Amaretti topping in small pieces over sweet potatoes and bake for 30 minutes.

Suggestion~
To make a day before serving, refrigerate the sweet potatoes and topping separately. Bring the sweet potatoes to room temperature before adding the topping.

# Cold Sides

~

# Broccoli Salad

*This salad, along with an Armenian flatbread roll-up of turkey, tomato, lettuce and a garlic-herb cream cheese spread, was Barry's favorite lunch to bring to the Sunday afternoon football games in the days of Candlestick. Go, Niners!!*

*Dressing:*
½ cup mayonnaise
2 tablespoons sugar
1 tablespoon fresh lemon juice or cider vinegar

*Salad:*
1 bunch broccoli, stalks peeled and roughly chopped
¼ cup diced red onion
¼ cup black currants or dried cranberries

Combine all dressing ingredients in a large bowl.

Add salad ingredients to the bowl with dressing. Combine well and refrigerate for an hour.


Suggestion~
Add cooked and crumbled bacon or chopped roasted peanuts.

The dressing may also be used for cole slaw or broccoli slaw.

# Orange and Cauliflower Salad

*Light and flavorful, this is a great offering in the winter when oranges and cauliflower are most abundant.*

*Vinaigrette:*
½ cup tarragon vinegar
finely grated zest of 2 oranges
¼ cup fresh orange juice
1 teaspoon dried basil
¾ teaspoon kosher salt
freshly ground black pepper, to taste
½ cup olive oil

*Salad:*
1 head cauliflower, cut into small florets
1 orange, segmented and cut into thirds
2 scallions, thinly sliced

Combine all vinaigrette ingredients, except oil, in a wide, rather than deep, container with lid. Cover and shake well. Add oil and shake again.

Steam florets until crisp tender. Drain and immerse in ice water to stop cooking. Drain and dry on towels, patting dry to absorb all water.

Add cauliflower, oranges and scallions to container with vinaigrette. Shake gently to distribute vinaigrette. Refrigerate for at least 4 hours, shaking periodically.

# Spinaci

*This is one of Barry's absolute favorites! It's also great as part of an antipasti platter or served hot as a side dish.*

2 tablespoons olive oil
3 garlic cloves, minced
1 pound spinach, thick stems removed
kosher salt
freshly ground black pepper

lemon wedges

Heat oil in a large skillet. Add garlic and stir for one minute.

Add a handful of spinach, using tongs to keep it moving as it cooks. As it begins to wilt, add another handful while moving the cooked spinach on top of the raw spinach. Continue adding a handful at a time, constantly moving the spinach, until the last batch added is almost wilted.

Remove from heat and add salt and pepper to taste. Rest pan on a slight angle and push spinach to the high side of pan allowing the liquid to accumulate on the low side. Press spinach to exude most of the liquid and transfer to a plate.

Refrigerate for about an hour; serve with lemon wedges.

# Cucumber Salad

½ cup unseasoned rice vinegar (preferably Marukan)
2 tablespoons + 2 teaspoons sugar
½ teaspoon kosher salt
1 tablespoon canola oil
chopped fresh dill or dried dill, to taste
3 English cucumbers, skin peeled alternately to create stripes, thinly sliced
¼ cup slivered red onion

Combine vinegar, sugar and salt in a wide, rather than deep, container with lid. Cover and shake well. Add oil and dill; shake again. Taste and adjust seasoning.

Add cucumbers and onion; shake to combine. Refrigerate at least four hours, shaking periodically.


# Tomatoes and Grilled Corn

¼ cup red wine vinegar
1 tablespoon canola oil
1 pint cherry tomatoes, halved
½ small red onion, diced
kosher salt, to taste
freshly ground black pepper, to taste
4 ears white corn

Combine all ingredients, except corn, in a large bowl. Husk and grill corn until lightly browned. Cut kernels off the corn as soon as it is cool enough to handle and combine with tomato mixture. Serve immediately.


Suggestion:
Add one diced avocado.

# Veggie~Stuffed Tomatoes

8 large beefsteak tomatoes
kosher salt
¼ cup olive oil
zest of 1 lime
2 tablespoons fresh lime juice
1 garlic clove, minced
2 tablespoons chopped shallots
2 tablespoons chopped cilantro leaves
kosher salt, to taste
freshly ground black pepper, to taste
2 ears white corn, kernels cut off
1 large red pepper, diced
1 small jalapeno, minced
1 avocado, diced

Cut tomatoes crosswise in half. Seed tomatoes and use a melon baller or other small spoon to scoop out the center of tomatoes; set aside. Sprinkle the inside of the tomato shells lightly with salt, then place upside-down on paper towels and let drain for 30 minutes.

Chop reserved tomato pulp and place in a strainer. Toss lightly with salt and let drain 15 minutes; set aside.

Whisk oil, lime zest and juice, garlic, shallots, cilantro, salt and pepper in a bowl.

Gently mix in remaining ingredients, including the chopped tomato pulp. Spoon corn salad into tomato shells. Cover and chill for up to 4 hours. Bring to room temperature before serving.

# Zucchini Ribbons

*Light and flavorful, this is from Julia's repertoire.*

*Vinaigrette:*
¼ cup fresh lemon juice
kosher salt, to taste
freshly ground black pepper, to taste
¼ teaspoon dried red pepper flakes
⅓ cup olive oil

*Zucchini:*
6 zucchini
kosher salt
½ cup chopped basil
½ cup chopped mint
Asiago, Pecorino Romano or Parmesan-Reggiano wedge

Combine all vinaigrette ingredients, except oil, in a container with a lid and shake. Add oil and shake again. Refrigerate several hours or overnight.

Starting at the outside of a zucchini, use a vegetable peeler or mandolin to cut zucchini into thin ribbons. Cut each of the 4 sides until you see the seeds. (Use the cores for another purpose.)

Place the ribbons of one zucchini on a double layer of paper towels or on a clean dishcloth. Sprinkle lightly with salt and cover with another layer of towels. Repeat the process with the remaining 5 zucchini. Place the stack on a plate and cover the top layer with towels. Cover plate with plastic wrap and refrigerate several hours or overnight.

Shortly before serving, gently toss zucchini with vinaigrette and herbs. Using a vegetable peeler, add cheese shavings to taste. Serve immediately.


Suggestion~
Add ⅓ cup toasted chopped pine nuts or walnuts.

# Applesauce

*You'll be amazed at how much tastier this is than the jarred variety... and it's super quick and easy to make!*

1 cup water
1½ tablespoons fresh lemon juice
¼ cup sugar
¼ teaspoon ground cinnamon
3 Granny Smith or other tart apples
2 McIntosh apples

Combine all ingredients, except apples, in a deep 2½-quart microwaveable casserole dish.

Peel apples and cut into 1" chunks. Add to casserole dish and stir to combine. Microwave on High for 5 minutes. Stir, pressing apples into liquid; microwave for an additional 5 minutes.

Use a potato masher and mash apples to the consistency you prefer.

Serve warm, room temperature or chilled.


Suggestion~
Sprinkle additional cinnamon on top when serving.

# Rum Lime Melon Balls

*These melons, loaded with flavor from the infused simple syrup, are an enjoyable change from the ubiquitous fruit salad.*

⅔ cup sugar
⅓ cup water
zest from 1 lime
¼ cup + 2 tablespoons fresh lime juice
⅓ cup light rum
1 tablespoon packed finely chopped mint leaves
1 cantaloupe, scooped into balls
1 honeydew, scooped into balls

In a small saucepan, combine sugar and water; bring to boil. Reduce heat and simmer 5 minutes. Remove from heat, add zest and cool completely. Stir in lime juice, rum and mint; set aside.

Place the melon balls in a large bowl. Add the rum-lime syrup and stir gently to coat the melon balls; refrigerate for at least 2 hours before serving, stirring occasionally.

# Watermelon Feta Salad

*This eclectic combination of flavors is from Julia. The juxtaposition of the sweet watermelon and the salty Feta, along with the fresh herbs and tart lime, is just sublime!*

*Vinaigrette:*
zest from 1 lime
¼ cup fresh lime juice
1 tablespoon honey
½ teaspoon salt
freshly ground black pepper, to taste
2½ tablespoons olive oil

*Salad:*
5 - 6 pound watermelon, cut into ½" cubes
kosher salt
3 mini cucumbers, thinly sliced
¼ cup diced red onion
¼ cup basil chiffonade
¼ cup mint chiffonade
¼ cup crumbled Feta

Combine all vinaigrette ingredients, except oil, in a container with lid. Shake well, then add oil; shake again. Refrigerate several hours or overnight.

Place watermelon in a colander set in a large bowl. Sprinkle lightly with salt, toss and repeat. Cover with plastic wrap and refrigerate all day or overnight.

Discard the watermelon juice from the bowl and transfer the watermelon to the same bowl. Add the cucumbers and onion. Shake the vinaigrette and combine with the salad. Gently stir in the herbs and Feta.

Suggestion~
To chiffonade leaves, stack the leaves, roll tightly from the long side and slice very thinly crosswise.

# Tabbouleh

*Vinaigrette:*
1 garlic clove, minced
⅓ cup fresh lemon juice
½ teaspoon freshly ground black pepper
½ teaspoon kosher salt
½ cup canola oil

*Salad:*
1 cup bulgur, rinsed and drained
½ cup chicken or vegetable broth, boiling
1 pint cherry tomatoes, halved
1 English cucumber, peeled, seeded and diced
½ cup packed chopped mint leaves
¼ cup chopped flat-leaf parsley leaves
3 scallions, finely chopped
⅓ cup pine nuts, toasted

~

Whisk all vinaigrette ingredients, except oil, in a bowl. Slowly whisk in oil; set aside.

Place bulgur in a large bowl; pour boiling broth over and stir periodically until broth is absorbed. Stir in vinaigrette, mixing well.

When cool, add remaining ingredients, except pine nuts, and refrigerate overnight. When ready to serve, stir in pine nuts. Taste and adjust seasonings.

Suggestion~
Add crumbled Feta.

Bulgur is a hearty grain and may be substituted with couscous (follow package directions) if a softer texture is preferred.

# Panzanella

½ cup balsamic vinegar
¼ cup + 3 tablespoons olive oil
1 garlic clove, minced
kosher salt, to taste
¼ teaspoon freshly ground black pepper + more for bread cubes
½ red onion, thinly sliced
2 pounds tomatoes, seeded and cut into chunks
½ loaf French bread
½ bunch basil leaves, chopped
8 ounces fresh mozzarella, cubed

Whisk vinegar, ¼ cup oil, garlic, salt and pepper in a large bowl. Add onion and let stand at room temperature for 30 minutes.

Place tomatoes in a colander; toss lightly with salt and let drain for 20 minutes, stirring periodically. Add tomatoes to the onions.

Preheat oven to 375°. Cut bread into 1" cubes. Pour 3 tablespoons oil onto a large rimmed baking sheet and season to taste with salt and pepper. Toss cubes in seasoned oil to lightly coat. Bake for 5 - 7 minutes, until crisp on the outside and soft in the center; let cool.

After tomatoes have marinated for 30 minutes, add toasted bread cubes and stir until bread is partially saturated, but not completely soaked through. Stir in basil and mozzarella. Serve immediately.

# Veggie, Black Bean and Rice Salad

*Vinaigrette:*
3 tablespoons orange juice
2 tablespoons red wine vinegar
2 teaspoons ground cumin
1 teaspoon chili powder
>½ teaspoon kosher salt
¼ teaspoon freshly ground black pepper
⅓ cup olive oil

*Salad:*
2 cups freshly cooked white rice
15-ounce can black beans, rinsed and drained
1 red pepper, chopped
1 yellow pepper, chopped
1 ear white corn, kernels cut off
15 cherry or grape tomatoes, quartered
½ red onion, diced
¼ cup finely chopped fresh cilantro leaves
1 avocado, diced

Whisk all vinaigrette ingredients, except oil, in a small bowl. Slowly whisk in oil and blend well. Taste and adjust seasoning.

Place the hot rice in a large bowl and fluff with a fork. Stir in vinaigrette while rice is hot, combining well. Stir occasionally while rice cools.

When rice is cool, add remaining ingredients, except avocado, and refrigerate at least 6 hours or overnight. Bring to room temperature before serving and gently stir in avocado.

# Veggie Couscous Salad

*When I first made this for the staff appreciation luncheon at the girls' elementary school, I used rice. After making it for years, I've found that couscous is much quicker than rice and just as delicious.*

*Vinaigrette:*
2 garlic cloves, minced
½ cup red wine vinegar
2 teaspoons sugar
2 teaspoons Dijon mustard
1 teaspoon freshly ground black pepper
½ teaspoon kosher salt
⅔ cup olive oil

*Salad:*
10-ounce box plain couscous
2 cups low-sodium chicken broth, boiling
½ teaspoon kosher salt
1 tablespoon olive oil
1 red pepper, diced
1 orange pepper, diced
1 pound asparagus, blanched and cut into 1" pieces
½ small red onion, finely diced
4 scallions, thinly sliced
¼ cup finely chopped flat-leaf parsley leaves
½ cup chopped fresh dill
1 cup frozen petite peas, thawed
1 cup dried black currants

Whisk all vinaigrette ingredients, except oil, in a small bowl and mix well. Slowly whisk in oil; set aside.

Place couscous in a large bowl and pour boiling broth, salt and oil over; stir and cover tightly. Let stand 5 minutes. Uncover couscous and stir in vinaigrette, mixing well. Stir couscous periodically, until cool.

Add remaining ingredients and refrigerate at least 6 hours. Bring to room temperature before serving.

# Boursin Potatoes

*Although this isn't strictly a 'cold' dish, it's akin to potato salad and would most likely be served in that context.*

3 pounds small red potatoes
5-ounce package garlic and herb Boursin cheese, room temperature
1½ teaspoons fresh lemon juice
3 tablespoons olive oil
kosher salt
freshly ground black pepper
¼ cup chopped flat-leaf parsley leaves

Place potatoes in a saucepan and fill with cold water and enough salt to be well-salted, taking care that water covers potatoes. Bring water to a boil over medium heat and cook until potatoes are just tender; drain and let cool a bit.

While potatoes cook, crumble cheese in a food processor work bowl; process until smooth. Add lemon juice and oil; process until blended. Season to taste with salt and pepper; stir in parsley.

Cut warm potatoes into chunks and gently stir in Boursin mixture until potatoes are coated; serve immediately.

# Thanksgiving

Baked Brie with Caramelized Onions • 160
Pumpkin Soup • 161
Brined Roasted Turkey • 162
Turkey Gravy • 163
Haricot Verts with Shallots • 164
Bread Stuffing • 165
Chestnut Stuffing • 166
Apricot Sweet Potatoes • 167
Cranberry Sauce • 168
Dessert • 169

~

# Baked Brie with Caramelized Onions

*While this certainly isn't an exclusively Thanksgiving recipe, we look forward to it every year as part of the hors d'oeuvre repertoire for our family's favorite holiday.*

2 tablespoons unsalted butter
4 large sweet yellow onions, sliced
1 teaspoon dried thyme leaves
4 garlic cloves, minced
½ cup good-quality dry white wine, divided
1 teaspoon sugar
kosher salt
freshly ground black pepper
1½ - 2 pound whole Brie, room temperature

1 baguette, thinly sliced and lightly toasted
Honey Crisp apples, sliced

Preheat oven to 350°. In a large skillet over medium-high heat, melt butter and sauté onions 5 minutes. Add thyme, reduce heat to medium and cook until onions are golden, stirring often, about 25 minutes. Add garlic and cook 2 minutes.

Add ¼ cup wine and stir until almost all liquid is evaporated, about 2 minutes. Sprinkle sugar over onions and cook until soft and brown, about 10 minutes.

Add remaining ¼ cup wine and stir another 2 minutes. Season to taste with salt and pepper.

Unwrap Brie and slice off top rind. Place in a baking dish as close the diameter of the Brie as possible. Top with onions.

Bake until Brie just melts, about 30 minutes. Let cool 10 minutes and serve with baguette and apple slices.

Suggestion~
The onions may be prepared 2 days in advance. Cool and refrigerate them until ready to proceed.

# Pumpkin Soup

*We visited a pumpkin patch every October so the girls could pick their pumpkins for Halloween. While they were choosing theirs, Barry and I would choose the pumpkin that we would serve this soup in. It had to be just the right size and shape so it would look perfect on our Thanksgiving table.*

¼ cup unsalted butter
1 large white onion, sliced
¾ cup sliced scallions, white and light green part only
16-ounce can pumpkin
3 14-ounce cans low-sodium chicken broth
1 bay leaf
½ teaspoon sugar
½ teaspoon curry powder
¼ teaspoon ground nutmeg
¼ cup packed flat-leaf parsley leaves

Melt butter in a 4-quart saucepan over medium-high heat and sauté onions until soft, but not brown. Add remaining ingredients. Bring to a boil, then reduce heat; simmer 15 minutes.

Discard bay leaf. Remove from heat and let cool 10 minutes. Purée soup with an immersion blender and reheat before serving.

Suggestion~
The soup may be prepared several days ahead; cool completely and refrigerate.

To serve in a pumpkin, hollow out a large pumpkin. When you're almost ready to serve the soup, fill about ⅔ of the pumpkin with water and microwave on High for 5 minutes. Check to see if the water is hot, and continue heating in 2-minute increments until it is hot. Let stand for several minutes to warm the pumpkin. Pour water out, place the pumpkin on a platter, fill with hot soup and serve immediately.

# Brined Roasted Turkey

25-pound turkey

*Brine:*
1 gallon orange juice
1 bottle white wine, such as Riesling or Sauvignon Blanc
2 cups kosher salt
2 cups sugar
2 oranges, quartered
2 lemons, quartered
2 heads garlic, sliced in half horizontally
1 small bunch each marjoram, rosemary and thyme
3 tablespoons whole black peppercorns

*Herb rub:*
olive oil
1 small bunch each rosemary and thyme, finely chopped

*Suggested aromatics:*
1 sweet yellow onion, quartered
1 orange, quartered
½ head garlic
rosemary or thyme sprigs

*Vegetable base:*
2 sweet yellow onions, quartered
2 pounds baby carrots
1 bunch celery, halved

4 cups low-sodium chicken broth

Remove turkey neck and bags from body cavity; discard. Rinse turkey well inside and out. Drain and dry inside and out with paper towels.

Combine all brine ingredients in a 5-gallon bucket. Immerse turkey in liquid and add enough cold water to cover turkey. Cover with plastic wrap and refrigerate for 24 - 30 hours.

Preheat oven to 325°. Remove turkey, discarding brine, and pat outside dry with paper towels. Rub just enough olive oil onto skin to moisten. Sprinkle with the chopped herbs. Fill the cavity with any or all of the aromatics.

Combine the vegetables in a large roasting pan. Place the turkey on top, and pour in enough broth to come halfway up the sides of the pan.

Roast the turkey for about 3½ hours, or until internal temperature measures 165°, basting every 30 minutes. Add broth as needed to maintain liquid level. Rotate the pan periodically so the turkey browns evenly. When the turkey is nicely browned, after 3 hours or so, tent with aluminum foil.

When the turkey is done, transfer it to a carving board. Allow it to rest at least 30 minutes before carving.


Suggestion~
A 5-gallon bucket can be found at a hardware store.

If refrigerator space is limited, improvise by placing the bucket in a large cooler and surrounding it with ice.

If cooking your turkey earlier in the day or even the day before is preferred, place the carved slices in a large pan. Remove the onions, carrots and celery from the roasting pan. Strain the cooked broth through a mesh strainer and pour over turkey slices until they are submerged, adding chicken broth, if needed. Cover with plastic wrap and refrigerate until 1½ hours before serving. Remove from refrigerator and let it sit at room temperature for 1 hour. Remove plastic wrap, cover with aluminum foil, and reheat at 325° for about 30 minutes, or until completely warmed through.


# Turkey Gravy

5 tablespoons turkey drippings
5 tablespoons all-purpose flour
14-ounce can low-sodium chicken broth
kosher salt
freshly ground black pepper

Heat drippings in a small saucepan over medium heat. Add flour and whisk about 3 minutes. Add broth very slowly and cook, whisking until thickened. Season to taste with salt and pepper.

# Haricots Verts with Shallots

*Thanksgiving side dishes traditionally include a number of heavy ones, such as stuffing and potatoes, so I like to accompany them with a simple vegetable that is crisp and green. These beans combine both of those elements.*

2 pounds haricots verts, ends trimmed
2 tablespoons unsalted butter
1 tablespoon olive oil
2 shallots, diced
kosher salt
freshly ground black pepper

Steam beans until crisp tender. Drain and immerse in ice water immediately to stop the cooking. Drain the beans and dry on towels.

Heat butter and oil in a skillet over medium-low heat and sauté shallots for 5 - 10 minutes, or until they are lightly browned.

Add beans to the pan and cook until beans are heated through. Season to taste with salt and pepper.

Suggestion~
To make this in advance, cook the beans as directed. Place the drained and dried beans in a zip-top bag and refrigerate up to 2 days. Bring them to room temperature before proceeding.

# Bread Stuffing

*This is easily everyone's favorite part of our Thanksgiving dinner…
we're even nibbling on it while cleaning up the kitchen! I usually
double the recipe to guarantee lots of leftovers.*

1½ pounds buttermilk, potato or other 'light' bread
1 cup unsalted butter
2 sweet yellow onions, chopped
2 cups diced celery
1¼ cups hot low-sodium chicken broth, divided
½ cup chopped flat-leaf parsley leaves
poultry seasoning (preferably Bell's seasoning)
kosher salt
freshly ground black pepper
2 large eggs, beaten
¼ cup turkey drippings

Toast bread and cool slices by standing up 2 slices so they touch at the top,
creating a tent; this will keep them crisp. When cool, make 3 even cuts
vertically and 3 horizontally, turning out 16 cubes per slice. Set aside in a
large bowl.

Preheat oven to 350°. In a large skillet over medium heat, melt butter and
sauté onions and celery about 5 minutes. Add ¼ cup hot broth and cover
pan for 10 minutes. Add remaining 1 cup broth and parsley.

Pour hot vegetables over bread cubes; mix well and season generously with
poultry seasoning. The poultry seasoning taste should be very pronounced,
as it will mellow with baking. Add salt and pepper to taste.

Stir in eggs, mixing well, and place in a well-greased 2½-quart casserole.
Drizzle top of stuffing with turkey drippings.

Cover with greased aluminum foil and bake for 45 minutes. Uncover and
bake an additional 10 minutes.


Suggestion~
The bread may be toasted and cubed early in the day. Place the cubes in a
large bowl and cover them loosely with aluminum foil until ready to use.

# Chestnut Stuffing

*I have fond memories of my mom and dad making this stuffing when I was growing up. After the chestnuts were boiled, we'd all sit around the kitchen table to help peel them. It's definitely a labor-intensive dish, but this stuffing is worth it!*

12 slices buttermilk, potato or other 'light' bread; enough to measure
  6 cups when cubed
2½ pounds chestnuts
½ cup unsalted butter
2 large sweet yellow onions, chopped
1 cup diced celery
¼ cup chopped flat-leaf parsley leaves
kosher salt
freshly ground black pepper
pinch dried thyme leaves
pinch ground ginger
low-sodium chicken broth, heated

~

Toast bread and cool slices by standing up 2 slices so they touch at the top, creating a tent; this will keep them crisp. When cool, make 3 even cuts vertically and 3 horizontally, turning out 16 cubes per slice. Set aside in a large bowl.

Cut an 'X' on the flat side of the chestnuts. Place them in a large pot and cover with cold water. Bring the water to a boil and boil for 15 minutes.

Remove from heat and set aside until the chestnuts are cool enough to handle. Hull and skin the chestnuts. Return them to boiling salted water and cook until soft. Drain the chestnuts and roughly mash them, keeping them somewhat chunky.

Preheat oven to 350°. In a skillet, melt butter and sauté the onions and celery until tender. Remove from heat and add parsley. Pour the hot vegetables over the toasted bread cubes. Add seasonings, to taste.

Mix in chestnuts and gradually add enough hot broth to moisten. Place in a greased casserole dish and bake at for 45 - 60 minutes.

# Apricot Sweet Potatoes

*While there is another sweet potato recipe offered in this book, I make this one the most frequently for Thanksgiving.*

8 orange-flesh sweet potatoes
¼ cup unsalted butter, room temperature
½ - ¾ cup light brown sugar, to taste
1 teaspoon ground cinnamon
1 cup dried apricots, finely diced
finely grated zest of 1 orange
1 orange, juiced

Preheat oven to 400°. Prick potatoes all over with a fork and place them on an aluminum foil-lined large rimmed baking sheet. Roast for about an hour, or until they are soft. Set them aside until cool enough to handle.

Reduce oven temperature to 375°. Split potatoes open; scoop the flesh into a large bowl and mash. Combine potatoes with remaining ingredients, in the order given, while potatoes are still warm. Transfer to a greased 3-quart casserole and bake for 40 minutes.


Suggestion~
This may be made one day in advance and refrigerated. Bring it to room temperature before baking.

# Cranberry Sauce

¾ cup water
1⅛ cups sugar
12-ounce bag fresh cranberries
½ cup apricot jam
2 tablespoons fresh lemon juice

In a 3-quart saucepan, boil water and sugar over medium heat, stirring until sugar is dissolved.

Add cranberries and cook until all pop. Press berries against the sides of the pan with the back of a spoon.

Remove from heat and add jam, stirring until melted. Add lemon juice. Cool to room temperature; refrigerate.

Serve at room temperature.


Suggestion~
This may be made several days in advance.

# Dessert

*There are many ways to go for Thanksgiving dessert, but I've made these most often. It's good to know that, on such a cooking-intensive day, some things may be made in advance. The page numbers for these recipes can found in the index.*

Apple Crisp – topping may be made ahead and frozen

Rustic Apple Pie – crust may be made ahead and refrigerated

Black Bottom Cupcakes – may be made ahead and frozen

Caramel Brownies – may be made ahead and frozen

Pecan Bars – may be made ahead and frozen

Mini Pecan Tarts – may be made ahead and frozen

Pumpkin Pie – best made one day in advance

# Brunches and Breads

~

# Green Chile Frittata

*This easy and delicious frittata is from my sister, Lauren. It also works well for a light dinner served with a green salad.*

½ cup all-purpose flour + more for dusting
1 teaspoon baking powder
1 teaspoon kosher salt
¼ teaspoon freshly ground black pepper
10 large eggs, beaten
6 tablespoons unsalted butter, melted and slightly cooled
2 cups small curd cottage cheese
8 ounces grated Cheddar and/or Jack cheese
3 4-ounce cans diced green chiles

salsa
sour cream
avocado

Preheat oven to 350°. Mix dry ingredients in a bowl. Add remaining ingredients and blend well.

Spray a 9" x 13" baking pan with cooking spray and dust lightly with flour. Pour frittata mixture into pan and bake for 35 - 45 minutes, or until set and lightly browned.

Let cool 10 minutes and cut into squares. May be served hot, warm or at room temperature.

Serve with salsa, sour cream and sliced avocado.


Suggestion~
The chiles and grated cheese may be substituted with chopped vegetables and
1 cup freshly grated Parmesan. Use vegetables such as asparagus, onions, red peppers, etc., that are not watery or too hard; they do not need to be cooked beforehand.

# Caramelized French Toast

*This is pretty rich, so small servings (Did I just say that?!) may be preferred. A slice would be a great accompaniment to scrambles and fresh fruit. You do have to love a dish that can be made the night before and popped into the oven in the morning... and tastes scrumptious!*

1 King's Hawaiian round bread
6 tablespoons unsalted butter
½ cup packed light brown sugar
1 tablespoon light corn syrup
6 large eggs
1 cup milk
1 tablespoon pure vanilla extract
1 tablespoon sugar
⅛ teaspoon salt

Slice bread in half and cut 6 slices from one of the halves; do not include ends. Wrap remaining half for another use. Dry bread by standing up 2 slices so they touch at the top, creating a tent. Allow tented bread to dry for several hours or all day.

In a small saucepan, melt butter with sugar and syrup over medium-low heat, stirring until sugar is dissolved and blends into the butter. Generously grease the sides of a 9" x 13" baking pan and pour sugar mixture in bottom of pan, spreading it quickly with the back of a spoon to evenly to coat the bottom.

While sugar mixture cools, beat eggs and mix with remaining ingredients until well blended. Pour some egg mixture over the sugar mixture. Arrange dried bread slices in the pan in a single layer and pour remaining egg mixture evenly over bread; turn slices over a few times so liquid absorbs into each slice. (It's okay if liquid does not absorb completely.) Cover with plastic wrap and refrigerate overnight.

Preheat oven to 350°. Remove plastic and cover with aluminum foil. Bake for 15 minutes; remove foil. Bake for an additional 20 - 25 minutes. Lift out with a spatula and flip onto a plate so the caramelized sugar is on top.

Suggestion~
If King's Hawaiian round bread is unavailable, challah is a good substitute.

# Orange French Toast

*Prepping this the night before cooking allows for a relaxing morning.*

1 King's Hawaiian round bread
4 large eggs
¾ cup milk
2 tablespoons Grand Marnier
1 tablespoon sugar
1 teaspoon pure vanilla extract
¼ teaspoon kosher salt
1 tablespoon unsalted butter + more, if needed

powdered sugar
maple syrup

Slice bread in half and cut 8 1" slices from one of the halves; do not include ends. Wrap remaining half for another use. Dry bread by standing up 2 slices so they touch at the top, creating a tent. Allow tented bread to dry for several hours or all day. Arrange the dried slices in a single layer in a 9" x 13" baking pan.

Beat eggs and combine with milk, Grand Marnier, sugar, vanilla and salt until well blended. Pour mixture evenly over bread; turn slices over a few times so liquid absorbs into each slice. Cover pan with plastic wrap and refrigerate overnight.

Preheat an electric griddle to 325° or heat a griddle pan over medium heat; melt butter, but do not let brown. Cook bread on each side until nicely browned.

Dust with powdered sugar and serve with maple syrup on the side.


Suggestion~
If King's Hawaiian round bread is unavailable, challah is a good substitute.

# Apple Pancake

*This is, by far, the most requested brunch dish in our family.*

4 large eggs
1 cup milk
1 teaspoon pure vanilla extract
1 cup all-purpose flour
2 tablespoons sugar
3 tablespoons unsalted butter, divided
4 Granny Smith apples, peeled and sliced
cinnamon sugar

Preheat oven to 425°. While the oven is heating, place eggs in a food processor work bowl and blend for 1 - 2 minutes, until pale and frothy. Add milk, vanilla, flour and sugar; blend another minute or two.

When oven is almost heated to temperature, place 2 tablespoons butter in a 9" x 13" baking pan and put it in the oven to melt, taking care it does not brown. When butter is almost melted, remove pan from the oven and carefully tilt it to coat the bottom and sides.

Place apple slices in the pan and toss to coat them with butter. Arrange apples evenly, pour batter over and immediately return to the oven.

Bake until almost set, about 15 minutes. Remove from oven, dot with remaining 1 tablespoon butter and sprinkle liberally with cinnamon sugar.

Return to oven to puff and brown, about 10 minutes.

# Dutch Baby

3 large eggs, room temperature
⅔ cup milk, room temperature
⅔ cup all-purpose flour
1 tablespoon sugar
1 teaspoon pure vanilla extract
⅛ teaspoon kosher salt
2 tablespoons unsalted butter, cut into pieces

lemon wedges
powdered sugar

Preheat oven to 450°. While the oven is heating, place eggs in a food processor work bowl and blend for 1 - 2 minutes, until pale and frothy. Add milk, flour, sugar, vanilla and salt; blend another minute or two.

When oven is almost heated to temperature, place butter in a 9″ glass pie plate and put it in the oven to melt, taking care it does not brown. When butter is almost melted, remove pan from the oven and carefully tilt it to coat the bottom and sides. Pour batter into the hot pan and immediately return to the oven.

Bake about 12 minutes, or until puffed and golden brown. Do not open oven door while baking or pancake may deflate.

Serve with lemon wedges and a liberal dusting of powdered sugar, with extra powdered sugar on the side.

# Bluebs
# aka Buttermilk Pancakes

*My family agrees that this is the quintessential buttermilk pancake.*
*Since I almost always make them with blueberries, we've always called*
*them bluebs!*

1 cup all-purpose flour
1 tablespoon sugar
1½ teaspoons baking powder
½ teaspoon baking soda
¾ teaspoon kosher salt
1 egg, beaten
1 cup buttermilk
¼ cup milk
2 tablespoons canola oil
2 teaspoons pure vanilla extract

maple syrup

Combine dry ingredients in a bowl. Add remaining ingredients and stir until just combined (a few lumps are okay).

Preheat an electric griddle to 350° or heat a non-stick griddle pan over medium heat. Using a ¼-cup dry measure, scoop batter and pour onto the hot griddle. When pancakes bubble on top and edges look dry, flip over and cook until browned underneath.

Serve with maple syrup.


Suggestion~
Scatter any of the following on each pancake when first poured onto the griddle or skillet:
fresh blueberries
diced bananas
chocolate chips

# Lemon Ricotta Pancakes

2 large eggs
1 cup ricotta
⅔ cup milk
¼ cup fresh lemon juice
¾ cup all-purpose flour
2½ tablespoons sugar
1 tablespoon baking powder
½ teaspoon ground nutmeg
¼ teaspoon kosher salt

maple syrup
fruit preserves of choice

In a large bowl, whisk eggs. Whisk in ricotta, milk and lemon juice. Add dry ingredients and whisk just until combined.

Preheat an electric griddle to 325° or heat a non-stick griddle pan over medium heat. Using a ¼-cup dry measure, scoop batter and pour onto the hot griddle. When pancakes bubble on top and edges look dry, flip over and cook until browned underneath.

Serve with maple syrup or fruit preserves.

Suggestion~
Scatter some blueberries on each pancake when first poured onto the griddle or skillet.

If you prefer a lemonier flavor, add the finely grated zest of 1 lemon to the batter.

# Blintz Soufflé

*As the name implies, this is a light and fluffy rendition of traditional cheese blintzes.*

*Filling:*
4 ounces cream cheese, room temperature
8 ounces small curd cottage cheese
1 egg yolk
1 tablespoon sugar
1 tablespoon all-purpose flour
1 teaspoon pure vanilla extract
½ teaspoon ground cinnamon

*Batter:*
3 large eggs
¾ cup sour cream
¼ cup milk
4 tablespoons unsalted butter, melted
1 teaspoon finely grated lemon zest
½ cup all-purpose flour
¼ cup sugar
1 teaspoon baking powder

Place all filling ingredients in a food processor work bowl and blend until smooth, scraping sides of work bowl once. Transfer mixture to a bowl; set aside. Do not wash work bowl.

Preheat oven to 350°. Place eggs, sour cream, milk, butter and lemon zest in the work bowl; process until smooth. Add dry ingredients; blend again until smooth.

Pour half the batter into a greased 8″ x 8″ baking pan. Drop small spoonfuls of the cheese mixture in evenly spaced rows on top of the batter. Pour the remaining batter on top.

Bake the soufflé for about 45 minutes, or until it is puffy and the edges begin to turn golden. Cool on a wire rack for 5 minutes and cut into squares.

Suggestion~
Serve with fruit preserves or Fresh Blueberry Sauce (page 180).

# Blintz Bake

*If you're short on prep time, using pre-made blintzes makes this is quick and easy.*

6 frozen blintzes, flavor of your preference
3 large eggs, beaten
4 tablespoons butter, melted
¾ cup sour cream
2 tablespoons sugar
2 tablespoons orange juice
1 teaspoon pure vanilla extract
ground cinnamon

Preheat oven to 350°. Place frozen blintzes in a greased baking pan.

Combine remaining ingredients, except cinnamon, and pour over blintzes. Sprinkle with cinnamon.

Bake for 45 - 60 minutes.


# Fresh Blueberry Sauce

*French toast, pancakes and blintzes are taken to a new level when served with this sauce.*

⅔ cup water
½ cup sugar
1 tablespoon cornstarch
1½ cups fresh blueberries
1 tablespoon fresh lemon juice

Combine water, sugar and cornstarch in a saucepan. Cook over medium heat until thickened, stirring constantly. If mixture begins to boil, lower heat a bit.

Add berries and reduce heat; simmer 5 minutes, stirring occasionally. Remove from heat and stir in lemon juice. Serve warm, not hot.

# Cinnamon Apples

*Try this for a good fruit alternative in the winter when the berries and stone fruits of summer are scarce.*

2 tablespoons unsalted butter
2 tablespoons light brown sugar, packed
3 Granny Smith apples, peeled and cut into 8 wedges
½ teaspoon ground cinnamon
pinch of ground nutmeg
1 tablespoon water

Melt butter and brown sugar in a large skillet over medium-high heat. Add apples, cinnamon and nutmeg. Sauté until they're softened, about 10 minutes.
Add water and stir for 1 - 2 minutes.


# Smashed Potatoes

*These are a welcome change from the usual breakfast potatoes.*

2 medium-size red potatoes
1 tablespoon butter
1 tablespoon olive oil
dried thyme leaves
kosher salt
freshly ground black pepper

Wrap each potato in wax paper and microwave both on High for about 8 minutes, or until a knife is easily inserted; set aside, keeping paper on.

Melt butter with oil in a skillet over medium-high heat. When mixture is hot, use your hand and gently smash down on each potato and flatten to about ½"; remove paper and place in the pan. Cook potatoes until they are browned and crispy on each side, seasoning to taste with thyme, salt and pepper.

# Crunchy Granola

¼ cup canola oil
¼ cup honey
¼ cup pure maple syrup
<¼ cup packed light brown sugar
1 teaspoon kosher salt
1 tablespoon pure vanilla extract
1½ teaspoons ground cinnamon
3 cups old-fashioned rolled oats
½ cup chopped pecans or walnuts
½ cup slivered almonds
⅓ cup unsweetened coconut flakes
¼ cup pumpkin seeds

Preheat oven to 300°. In a small saucepan, combine oil, honey, maple syrup, brown sugar and salt. Cook over medium-low heat, stirring occasionally, until mixture begins to simmer. Remove from heat; stir in vanilla and cinnamon.

While liquids are heating, combine oats, nuts, coconut and pumpkin seeds in a large bowl. Pour the hot liquid over the oat mixture, stirring to combine well.

Spread granola evenly onto a parchment-lined large rimmed baking sheet and bake for 45 minutes, stirring every 15 minutes.

Cool baking sheet on a wire rack, stirring granola few times as it cools. (If you prefer granola clusters, do not stir while cooling.) When completely cooled, store in an airtight container.


Suggestion~
When granola is cool, mix in 1 cup dried fruit, such as apricots, blueberries, cherries, cranberries, etc. chopped to desired size.

Granola can be easily modified to suit your family's tastes. The type of nuts and seeds can be changed, as can the level of sweetness. Make it your own!

# Blueberry Muffins

*This has been Laura's favorite summer breakfast treat ever since she was a little girl. They're best enjoyed while warm.*

2 cups all-purpose flour, less 1 tablespoon
1 cup sugar
2 teaspoons baking powder
1½ teaspoons ground cinnamon
½ teaspoon kosher salt
2 large eggs
½ cup unsalted butter, melted and cooled
½ cup milk
1 teaspoon pure vanilla extract
1 pint blueberries, tossed with 1 tablespoon all-purpose flour

Preheat oven to 400°. Mix dry ingredients in a bowl. In a separate bowl, beat eggs and combine with remaining ingredients, except blueberries.

Stir egg mixture into flour mixture until just combined. Fold in blueberries.

Spray a 12-cup muffin pan with cooking spray and fill cups evenly with batter. Bake for about 20 minutes. Cool the pan on a wire rack for 10 minutes, then run a table knife along the sides before removing muffins.

# Popovers

1 cup all-purpose flour
¼ teaspoon kosher salt
1 cup milk
3 large eggs, beaten
½ cup grated Cheddar cheese
3 tablespoons unsalted butter, divided

~

Preheat oven to 375°. In a bowl, mix flour and salt. Slowly blend in milk; add eggs and cheese.

Place 1½ teaspoons of butter in each of 6 6-ounce Pyrex custard cups. Place cups on a rimmed baking sheet and, when the oven is almost heated to temperature, place the pan in the oven to melt butter, taking care it does not brown. When butter is melted, fill the cups evenly with batter and return to the oven immediately.

Bake for 45 - 50 minutes, or until they are well popped and browned. Do not open oven door while baking or popovers may deflate.

Slide a table knife down the sides and lift popover out of cup. Serve immediately.

# Gougères

*These classic French cheese puffs, made using pâte à choux, are a welcome change from the ubiquitous rolls or bread served with dinner. They may also be made smaller and offered as an appetizer. The earliest recipes for gougères, from France's Burgundy region, date back to the eighteenth century.*

½ cup water
4 tablespoons unsalted butter, cut into pieces
½ teaspoon kosher salt
a few grindings of black pepper or generous pinch of cayenne
½ cup flour
2 large eggs
½ cup grated Gruyère or Cheddar cheese

Preheat oven to 400°. In a 3-quart saucepan over medium-high heat, bring water, butter, salt and pepper to a full boil. Add flour all at once and, using a wooden spoon, quickly stir until the dough forms a ball. Remove pan from heat and let mixture cool about 2 minutes.

Beat in eggs one at a time, stirring vigorously until each is fully incorporated into the dough. Stir in cheese and blend well.

Place 6 equal-size mounds of dough onto a parchment-lined cookie sheet. Bake for about 35 minutes, or until well puffed and browned.

Serve immediately.

# Orange Cranberry Bread

*The flavors of this bread make it a perfect breakfast treat, mid-day or late night snack, particularly in November and December when cranberries are at their peak.*

2 cups all-purpose flour
1 cup sugar
1½ teaspoons baking powder
1 teaspoon kosher salt
½ teaspoon baking soda
1 egg
¾ cup fresh orange juice
2 tablespoons canola oil
1 tablespoon finely grated orange zest
12-ounce bag fresh cranberries

Preheat oven to 350°. Mix dry ingredients in a bowl and make a well in the center; add egg and beat. Add orange juice, oil and orange zest, mixing well. Stir in cranberries.

Place in a greased 9" x 5" loaf pan; bake for about 55 minutes, or until a tester inserted in the center comes out clean. Cool in pan on a wire rack for 15 minutes and run a table knife around sides. Remove from pan and cool completely on a different wire rack.

Wrap tightly in plastic wrap when cool.

Flavor improves after a day or two.


Suggestion~
Add ½ cup chopped toasted pecans.

# Pumpkin Bread

*As soon as autumn is in the air, Julia has cravings for this bread!*

3⅓ cups all-purpose flour
2 teaspoons baking soda
1½ teaspoons kosher salt
2 teaspoons ground cinnamon
1 teaspoon ground nutmeg
2½ cups sugar
4 large eggs
1 cup canola oil
⅔ cup water
16-ounce can pumpkin
½ cup chopped toasted pecans
½ cup dried cranberries

Preheat oven to 350°. Combine dry ingredients in a large bowl. Make a well in the center; add eggs and beat. Add oil, water and pumpkin and blend well. Stir in pecans and cranberries.

Pour into 2 greased and floured 9" x 5" loaf pans and bake for about 1 hour, or until a tester inserted in the center comes out clean. Cool in the pans on a wire rack for about 10 minutes, then run a table knife around sides. Remove from the pans and finish cooling on a different wire rack.

Wrap tightly in plastic wrap when cool.

# Poppy Seed Bread

*The glaze is what takes this bread from ordinary to extraordinary.*

*Bread:*
3 cups all-purpose flour
2 cups sugar
1½ tablespoons poppy seeds
1½ teaspoons baking powder
½ teaspoon kosher salt
3 large eggs, room temperature
1½ cups canola oil
1½ cups milk
1½ teaspoons pure vanilla extract
1½ teaspoons almond extract

*Glaze:*
⅓ cup sugar
2 tablespoons orange juice
¼ teaspoon almond extract

Preheat oven to 350°. Combine dry ingredients in a large bowl. Make a well in the center; add eggs and beat. Add remaining bread ingredients and blend well.

Pour into 2 greased 9" x 5" loaf pans. Bake for 50 - 55 minutes, or until a tester comes out clean. Cool in pans on a wire rack about 10 minutes and run a table knife around sides. Remove from pan and finish cooling on a different wire rack. Allow bread to cool for 30 minutes.

Place a sheet of aluminum foil under the rack. Combine all glaze ingredients and drizzle slowly over the warm bread, using the back of a spoon to spread the glaze; cool completely.

Wrap tightly in plastic wrap when cool. Tastes best a day after baking.

# Rustic Bread

2 cups lukewarm water
1 package dry yeast
1 tablespoon sugar
2 teaspoons kosher salt
1½ teaspoons dried rosemary leaves or other dried herbs
4 cups bread flour
1 tablespoon cornmeal
melted unsalted butter

Pour water into a large bowl. Sprinkle yeast, sugar and salt over; stir until dissolved. Stir in rosemary and flour. Transfer dough to a floured plate.

Clean the bowl and grease with butter. Return dough to the bowl and cover with a damp towel. Let rise in a warm place until doubled in bulk, about 45 minutes.

Grease a baking sheet and sprinkle it with cornmeal. Divide the dough in half and shape each half into an oblong loaf. Place the loaves on the baking sheet and let rise another 45 minutes until almost doubled.

Preheat oven to 425°. Brush loaves with melted butter and bake 10 minutes. Reduce oven temperature to 375° and bake an additional 20 minutes. Transfer to a wire rack to cool.

Serve warm.

# Sweets

*Continued...*

~

# A Cookie Note

Frozen scoops of cookie dough are known in our family as "Lumps." I've been making Lumps of different varieties since the girls were little. I started with a classic Chocolate Chip cookie, which has evolved over the years. I now include others, such as White Chocolate Chip Chocolate, Chocolate Chip and Cherry, and Cranberry Oatmeal. Everyone in my family seems to have a particular favorite and when they come to visit I send them home with a bagful and a freezer pack.

My Lumps are made by using a 1¾" diameter spring-loaded scoop. There are several scoop sizes available, so you can choose a size that fits your family's preferences. If you prefer, like I do, to bake a few cookies at a time rather than an entire batch, scoop the dough and place the Lumps on a rimmed baking sheet; freeze for about an hour. When frozen, transfer the Lumps to a freezer zip-top bag and store in the freezer. They can be baked while frozen; just add a few more minutes to the baking time. Another option, which my family seems to like, is to eat them right out of the bag!

# Lumps
# aka Chocolate Chip Cookies

1 cup unsalted butter, room temperature
1 cup sugar
1 cup packed light brown sugar
2 large eggs, room temperature
>1 teaspoon pure vanilla extract
2 cups all-purpose flour
1½ cups ground old-fashioned rolled oats
1 teaspoon baking powder
1 teaspoon baking soda
1 teaspoon kosher salt
12-ounce package semi-sweet chocolate chips

Preheat oven to 350°. In the bowl of a stand mixer, beat butter and sugars on medium-high speed until light and fluffy, scraping down sides as needed. Reduce speed to medium and add eggs and vanilla; blend thoroughly.

Combine dry ingredients and, on low speed, add to butter mixture, blending until combined. Add chips on lowest speed.

Using a spring-loaded scoop, scoop dough into Lumps. Place Lumps on a parchment-lined cookie sheet. Bake for about 10 minutes, or until done as desired. Transfer cookies to a wire rack to cool.


Suggestion~
For ground oats, place oats, in batches, in a food processor work bowl and process until ground. Grinding an entire carton allows it to be handy for the next batch made.

Add chopped and toasted walnuts or sweetened shredded coconut.

If you would prefer to freeze the dough, see A Cookie Note (page 193).

# White Chocolate Chip Chocolate Cookies

*The double chocolate flavor is what makes these Laura's favorite!*

1 cup unsalted butter, room temperature
¾ cup sugar
⅔ cup packed light brown sugar
2 large eggs, room temperature
1 teaspoon pure vanilla extract
2¼ cups all-purpose flour
⅔ cup unsweetened cocoa powder
1 teaspoon baking soda
½ teaspoon kosher salt
12-ounce package white chocolate chips

Preheat oven to 350°. In the bowl of a stand mixer, beat butter and sugars on medium-high speed until light and fluffy, scraping down sides as needed. Reduce speed to medium and add eggs and vanilla; blend thoroughly.

Combine dry ingredients and, on low speed, add to butter mixture, blending until combined. Add chips on lowest speed.

Using a spring-loaded scoop, scoop dough into Lumps. Place Lumps on a parchment-lined cookie sheet and bake for 8 - 10 minutes, or until done as desired. Transfer cookies to a wire rack to cool.


Suggestion~
If you would prefer to freeze the dough, see A Cookie Note (page 193).

# Chocolate Chip and Cherry Cookies

1 cup unsalted butter, room temperature
1 cup packed light brown sugar
½ cup sugar
2 large eggs, room temperature
1 tablespoon pure vanilla extract
2½ cups all-purpose flour
½ teaspoon baking soda
½ teaspoon kosher salt
12-ounce package semi-sweet chocolate chips
1 cup dried tart cherries

Preheat oven to 350°. In the bowl of a stand mixer, beat butter and sugars on medium-high speed until light and fluffy, scraping down sides as needed. Reduce speed to medium and add eggs and vanilla; blend thoroughly.

Combine dry ingredients and, on low speed, add to butter mixture, blending until combined. Add chips and cherries on lowest speed.

Using a spring-loaded scoop, scoop dough into Lumps. Place Lumps on a parchment-lined cookie sheet and bake for 8 - 10 minutes, or until done as desired. Transfer cookies to a wire rack to cool.

Suggestion~
If you would prefer to freeze the dough, see A Cookie Note (page 193).

# Cranberry Oatmeal Cookies

*Julia's absolute favorite cookie, especially warm right out of the oven with a glass of cold milk!*

1 cup unsalted butter, room temperature
1 cup packed light brown sugar
½ cup sugar
2 large eggs, room temperature
1 teaspoon pure vanilla extract
1½ cups all-purpose flour
1 teaspoon ground cinnamon
1 teaspoon baking soda
½ teaspoon kosher salt
3 cups whole old fashioned oats
1 cup unsweetened dried cranberries
½ cup chopped toasted walnuts

Preheat oven to 350°. In the bowl of a stand mixer, beat butter and sugars on medium-high speed until light and fluffy, scraping down sides as needed. Reduce speed to medium and add eggs and vanilla; blend thoroughly.

Combine dry ingredients and, on low speed, add to butter mixture, blending until combined. Add cranberries and walnuts on lowest speed.

Using a spring-loaded scoop, scoop dough into Lumps. Place Lumps on a parchment-lined cookie sheet and bake for 8 - 10 minutes, or until done as desired. Transfer cookies to a wire rack to cool.

Suggestion~
If you would prefer to freeze the dough, see A Cookie Note (page 193).

# Cinnamon Sugar Cookies

1 cup unsalted butter, room temperature
2 cups sugar
2 large eggs, room temperature
2 teaspoons pure vanilla extract
2¼ cups all-purpose flour
1 tablespoon + 1 teaspoon ground cinnamon
2 teaspoons baking powder
½ teaspoon kosher salt

Preheat oven to 350°. In the bowl of a stand mixer, beat butter and sugar on medium-high speed until light and fluffy, scraping down sides as needed. Reduce speed to medium and add eggs and vanilla, blending thoroughly.

Combine dry ingredients and, on low speed, add to butter mixture, blending until combined.

Using a spring-loaded scoop, scoop dough into Lumps. Place Lumps on a parchment-lined cookie sheet and bake for about 12 minutes, or until done as desired. Transfer cookies to a wire rack to cool.


Suggestion~
If you would prefer to freeze the dough, see A Cookie Note (page 193).

# Chocolate Crackles

1 cup semi-sweet chocolate chips
1 cup packed light brown sugar
5 tablespoons unsalted butter
2 large eggs, room temperature
1 teaspoon pure vanilla extract
1 cup all-purpose flour
1 teaspoon baking powder
¼ teaspoon kosher salt
½ cup powdered sugar

Melt chips, sugar and butter in a saucepan over medium-low heat. Transfer to a large bowl and let cool to lukewarm. Beat in eggs one at a time, blending well. Add vanilla.

In a separate bowl, combine flour, powder and salt; add to the chocolate mixture and blend well. Divide the dough between two bowls, cover and refrigerate at least 3 hours or overnight.

Take one bowl with dough from the refrigerator and scoop the dough using a 1¼″ diameter spring-loaded scooper. Place the lumps close together on a cookie sheet. Repeat with remaining dough. Cover lumps with plastic wrap and refrigerate at least 3 hours or overnight.

Preheat oven to 350°. Place the cold lumps in a large zip-top bag and add the powdered sugar. Seal the bag and shake so all lumps are coated with sugar. Place them on parchment-lined cookie sheets, spacing about 2″ apart.

Bake for 10 minutes, taking care not to over bake; cookies will firm up as they cool. Transfer cookies to a wire rack to cool completely.


Suggestion~
If you don't have a scooper, roll the dough into small walnut-size balls. Work quickly, as the heat from your hands will soften the dough.

The lumps can be frozen and thawed overnight in the refrigerator before being coated with the powdered sugar.

# Chocolate-Dipped Butter Cookies

1 cup unsalted butter, room temperature
¾ cup sugar
2 large egg yolks
1½ teaspoons pure vanilla extract
2¼ cups all-purpose flour
¼ teaspoon kosher salt
8 ounces semi-sweet chocolate, broken into 1" pieces if in bar form

In the bowl of a stand mixer, beat butter for 1 minute on medium-high speed, then add sugar and continue beating until light and fluffy. Reduce speed to medium and add egg yolks, then vanilla, scraping down sides as needed to blend thoroughly.

Combine flour and salt and add on low speed, blending until just combined. Divide dough in half and shape into logs; wrap in plastic wrap. Refrigerate for 2 - 3 hours.

Preheat oven to 350°. Remove one log from the refrigerator and slice dough into ¼" rounds, placing them on a parchment-lined cookie sheet. Repeat with the second log. Bake for 10 - 12 minutes, or until the bottoms are golden. Transfer cookies to a wire rack to cool completely.

Place a sheet of wax paper or aluminum foil under the wire rack. Place chocolate in a small microwaveable bowl and heat on High for 1 minute; stir until melted completely. Tip the bowl a bit and dip the top of the cookie halfway into chocolate; gently shake off excess. Place the dipped cookie back on the rack and let chocolate set before serving.


Suggestion~
The logs can be frozen, for baking later, by wrapping them tightly in plastic wrap, then aluminum foil. Store in a freezer zip-top bag. For ease of slicing, place a wrapped log in the refrigerator overnight to thaw.

As an alternative, create sandwich cookies by placing a bit of either melted chocolate or fruit jam between two plain cookies.

# Little Gems

1½ cups unsalted butter, room temperature
1 cup sugar
2 egg yolks
2 teaspoons pure vanilla extract
3 cups all-purpose flour
¼ teaspoon kosher salt
strawberry jam
about 2 cups pecan halves

Preheat oven to 325°. In the bowl of a stand mixer, beat butter and sugar on medium-high speed until light and fluffy. Reduce speed to medium and add egg yolks one at a time, scraping down sides as needed to blend thoroughly. Add vanilla, beating to combine.

Combine flour and salt and add on low speed, blending until combined.

Pinch off roll into 1" balls; place on a parchment-lined cookie sheet. Using the back of a rounded ½-teaspoon measure, make an indentation in the center. Place a small amount of jam in it and top with 1 pecan, pressing so it will adhere.

Bake for 15 minutes, or until pale golden on bottom. Transfer cookies to a wire rack to cool.

# Chocolate Thumbprints

*Filling:*
¾ cup semi-sweet chocolate chips
1 tablespoon unsalted butter, room temperature
2 tablespoons corn syrup
1 tablespoon water
1 teaspoon pure vanilla extract

*Dough:*
1 cup unsalted butter, room temperature
1 cup packed light brown sugar
2 teaspoons pure vanilla extract
4 tablespoons milk, room temperature
3 cups all-purpose flour
½ teaspoon kosher salt

Place chips and butter in a microwavable bowl. Microwave on High for 30 seconds. Stir until chips and butter are melted and blended. Cool slightly. Stir in remaining filling ingredients and set aside, for about one hour, to thicken.

Preheat oven to 375°. In the bowl of a stand mixer, beat butter and sugar on medium-high speed until light and fluffy.

Reduce speed to medium and add vanilla and milk, scraping down sides as needed to blend thoroughly. Combine flour and salt and add on low speed, blending until combined.

Pinch off dough and roll it into 1" balls; place on a parchment-lined cookie sheet. Using the back of a rounded ½-teaspoon measure, make an indentation in the center of each cookie. Place filling in a plastic zip-top freezer bag. Clip the corner to create a very small opening and gently squeeze some filling into each indentation.

Bake for 10 - 12 minutes. Transfer cookies to a wire rack to cool.

# Cut~Out Cookies

1 cup unsalted butter, room temperature
1½ cups sugar
2 large eggs, room temperature
1 tablespoon pure vanilla extract
3 cups all-purpose flour
2 teaspoons baking powder
½ teaspoon kosher salt

In the bowl of a stand mixer, beat butter and sugar on medium-high speed until light and fluffy. Reduce speed to medium and add eggs and vanilla, scraping down sides as needed to blend thoroughly.

Combine dry ingredients and, on low speed, add to butter mixture, blending until just combined. Divide dough in half. Flatten dough into disks and wrap individually in plastic wrap; refrigerate for 1 hour.

Preheat oven to 350°. On a lightly floured surface, roll out one disk to about ¼" thick. Cut out desired shapes with cookie cutters and place on a parchment-lined cookie sheet. Decorate, if desired. Bake for 6 - 8 minutes, or until golden. Repeat with second disk. Transfer baked cookies to a wire rack to cool.

# Lemon Rosemary Cookies

*These savory and not-overly-sweet cookies are my lemon-loving sister Linda's signature cookie.*

1 cup unsalted butter, room temperature
¾ cup sugar
1 egg
1 teaspoon pure vanilla extract
3 tablespoons fresh lemon juice
finely grated zest of 2 lemons
1 tablespoon chopped fresh rosemary
2¼ cups all-purpose flour
½ teaspoon kosher salt
1 egg white, beaten
decorators or sanding sugar

In the bowl of a stand mixer, beat butter and sugar on medium-high speed until light and fluffy. Reduce speed to medium and add egg, vanilla and lemon juice, scraping down sides as needed to blend thoroughly. Mix in lemon zest and rosemary.

Combine flour and salt; add on low speed, blending until combined.

Lay out 2 sheets of plastic wrap. Divide dough in half and place each half on the plastic. Form into a log as best you can (dough will be soft). Roll log up in the plastic and refrigerate for 1 hour.

Working with one log at a time, place unwrapped log on a work surface and roll it a bit so it is smooth and even in diameter. Roll it in a new piece of plastic wrap and freeze for 1 hour. Repeat with second log.

Preheat oven to 375°. Lay out a sheet of wax paper about 8" longer than the length of the log and place a heavy line of decorator's sugar, the length of the log, on the paper. Using a pastry brush or your hands, cover the log with egg white and immediately roll it in the decorator's sugar, pressing gently to adhere.

Slice ¼" rounds and place on a parchment-lined cookie sheet. Bake for about 13 - 14 minutes, or until the bottoms are golden brown. Transfer cookies to a wire rack to cool.

Suggestion~
The logs may be frozen for baking later, by wrapping them tightly in plastic wrap, then aluminum foil. Store in a freezer zip-top bag. For ease of slicing, place wrapped log in the refrigerator overnight to thaw.

# Mexican Wedding Cookies

1 cup unsalted butter, room temperature
1 cup sifted powdered sugar, divided
1½ teaspoons pure vanilla extract
2 cups all-purpose flour
¼ teaspoon kosher salt
¾ cup finely chopped pecans

In the bowl of a stand mixer, beat butter and sugar on medium-high speed until light and fluffy; add vanilla.

Add flour and salt on low speed, blending until partially combined. Add pecans and blend until the dough clumps together.

Preheat oven to 350°. Scoop the dough using a 1¼" diameter spring-loaded scooper (or use your hands and roll into walnut-size balls) and place the cookies on a parchment-lined cookie sheet, spacing about 1½" apart. Bake for about 12 minutes, or until set and the bottoms are light brown. Place a sheet of wax paper under a wire rack, then transfer cookies to the rack; cool for about 5 minutes.

While cookies are still warm, place ½ cup powdered sugar in a bowl and roll the warm cookies, one at a time, in the sugar. Place rolled cookies back on wire rack to cool completely.

Suggestion~
If you don't have a 1¼" diameter spring-loaded scooper, refrigerate the dough for 1 hour, then roll into 1" balls and proceed with the recipe.

# Fortune Cookies

*"...in bed!"*

1 egg
⅓ cup sugar
⅓ cup all-purpose flour
3 tablespoons canola oil + more for griddle
2 tablespoons water
½ teaspoon pure vanilla extract

Cut paper strips 3" x ½"; write a fortune on each strip.

Preheat an electric griddle to 350°. Beat egg until frothy and add sugar, blending well. Stir in remaining ingredients.

Brush a bit of oil onto the griddle. When hot, drop 1 tablespoon of batter on the griddle. Using the back of a spoon, quickly spread into a 3½" circle; cookie must be very thin. Repeat to cook several cookies at once.

Cook until light brown, about 3 minutes. Flip it over and cook an additional 3 minutes.

Have a muffin pan next to you. Quickly take one cookie at a time from the griddle, place a fortune in center and fold in half. Holding the edges, draw the cookie down over the edge of a muffin cup to crease in half. Fit the cookie into the muffin cup to hold its shape until it cools.

# Rugelach

*Dough:*
1 cup unsalted butter
8-ounce package cream cheese
¼ cup sugar
1 teaspoon vanilla
2 cups all-purpose flour
½ teaspoon kosher salt

*Filling:*
¾ cup sugar
¾ cup light brown sugar, packed
1 teaspoon ground cinnamon
1 cup finely chopped toasted walnuts
½ cup apricot jam, warmed slightly in the microwave to liquefy a bit

~

In the bowl of a stand mixer, cream the butter and cream cheese on medium-high speed. Blend in the sugar and vanilla. On low speed, add the flour and salt until just combined; dough will be moist. Form the dough into a ball, place it on a floured surface and divide it into fourths. Shape each quarter into a ball, then flatten it into a disk, wrapping each individually in plastic wrap; refrigerate for 1 hour.

Preheat oven to 350°. Combine sugars and cinnamon for the filling; set aside. Take out one disk of dough and let it sit at room temperature for 5 minutes. Roll out dough on a lightly floured surface to an 11″ - 12″ diameter circle. Thinly spread 2 tablespoons jam over the dough to cover it completely. (An offset spatula works well.) Sprinkle 3 tablespoons cinnamon sugar, then ¼ cup walnuts, evenly over the jam. Place a piece of wax paper over the filling and gently press nuts in.

Cut the circle into quarters, then cut each quarter into 4 wedges. (A pizza cutter works well.) Roll up each wedge from the wide end and place on a parchment-lined cookie sheet, with the point on the bottom. Curve the ends down to create a crescent shape. Repeat with remaining disks. Bake for about 25 - 27 minutes. Transfer to a wire rack to cool.

Suggestion~
The apricot jam may be substituted with seedless raspberry jam. Optional additions can be black currants, dried cranberries or shredded coconut.

# Fudgy Brownies

*These are the most requested brownies in our family. I've made them so often that the recipe is nearly obliterated with chocolate!*

1 cup unsalted butter, room temperature
2 cups sugar
2 teaspoons pure vanilla extract
4 large eggs, room temperature
4 1-ounce squares unsweetened chocolate, melted and cooled a bit
1 cup all-purpose flour
¼ teaspoon kosher salt

powdered sugar

Preheat oven to 325°. In the bowl of a stand mixer, beat butter and sugar on medium-high speed until light and fluffy. Reduce speed to medium and add eggs and vanilla, scraping down sides as needed to blend thoroughly. Blend in chocolate.

Combine flour and salt and add on low speed, blending until just combined.

Pour into a lightly greased 9" x 13" baking pan. Bake for about 35 minutes, or until top is dry and just beginning to crack. Cool in the pan on a wire rack. When cool, dust with powdered sugar and cut as desired.

Best made one day before serving.

# Caramel Brownies

*Laura has known her husband since they were kids, although they didn't begin dating until several years after college. Darren remembers coming over to our house when they were in high school and having caramel brownies. Now that they're married, he can enjoy them a lot more frequently!*

36 soft caramels
1 5-ounce can evaporated milk, divided
1 box German chocolate cake mix (preferably Betty Crocker)
½ cup unsalted butter, melted

Preheat oven to 350°. Place the caramels and half the milk in a microwaveable bowl. Heat on High for 2 minutes, stirring halfway. Stir until caramels and milk are completely incorporated; set aside.

In the bowl of a stand mixer, combine cake mix, butter and remaining milk on medium speed. Press half the mixture into an ungreased 9" x 13" baking pan. Bake for 6 minutes.

Remove pan from the oven. Pour melted caramels over the cake, evenly covering the surface and carefully spreading almost to the edge of the pan. Taking walnut-size pieces of remaining batter, press them between your palms to flatten and layer them over the caramel to cover the surface completely. (It will look like a messy patchwork.) Bake for an additional 15 minutes. Cool in the pan on a wire rack and cut as desired.

Suggestion~
For a salted caramel and chocolate taste, sprinkle some flaky sea salt over the top layer of batter before returning the pan to the oven.

# Blondies

*These are best the day they're made, especially when they're still warm from the oven.*

1½ cups unsalted butter
1 cup packed light brown sugar
½ cup packed dark brown sugar
2 large eggs, room temperature
1½ teaspoons pure vanilla extract
1½ cups all-purpose flour
1 teaspoon baking powder
½ teaspoon kosher salt
12-ounce package semi-sweet chocolate chips

Preheat oven to 325°. In a small saucepan, melt butter over medium-low heat. Add sugars and whisk until well blended with butter, about 15 minutes. Transfer to a bowl and let cool until lukewarm.

In a separate bowl, whisk eggs and vanilla, then whisk them into the butter-sugar mixture. Stir in dry ingredients until just combined. Stir in chips.

Place in a greased 9" x 13" baking pan and bake for about 28 - 30 minutes, taking care not to over bake. Cool in the pan on a wire rack and cut as desired.


Suggestion~
Add ½ cup chopped toasted walnuts or pecans.

# Brown Sugar Chocolate Chip Bars

2 cups packed light brown sugar
2 cups flour
½ cup unsalted butter, diced and frozen for 20 minutes
1 large egg
1 cup milk
1 teaspoon baking soda
1 teaspoon kosher salt
1 teaspoon pure vanilla extract
1 cup semi-sweet chocolate chips

Preheat oven to 325°. Place sugar and flour in a food processor work bowl and process to blend. Add butter and pulse until crumbly. Remove 1 cup of crumbs for topping; set aside.

Add remaining ingredients, except chips, to the work bowl. Process again until well blended, scraping the sides and bottom.

Transfer the batter to a greased 9" x 13" baking pan. Sprinkle with reserved crumbs and chips; press in gently. Bake for 30 - 35 minutes, taking care not to over bake. Cool in the pan on a wire rack and cut as desired.


Suggestion~
Add ½ chopped toasted walnuts or pecans to the topping.

# Coconut Chocolate Chip Bars

*My husband's love of food began as a child when he first tasted coconut. Even after indulging in these bars for so many years, they still bring a big smile to his face.*

½ cup unsalted butter, melted
1½ cups graham cracker crumbs
14-ounce can sweetened condensed milk
12-ounce package semi-sweet chocolate chips
1⅓ cups sweetened shredded coconut

Preheat oven to 350°. Using a fork, combine butter and crumbs in a bowl. Grease the sides of a 9" x 13" baking pan and press crumbs evenly into the bottom of the pan.

Pour milk evenly over the crumb mixture. Scatter chips and coconut over the milk. Press in lightly with a fork.

Bake for 25 minutes. Cool in the pan on a wire rack and cut as desired.

# Pecan Bars

*Crust:*
⅓ cup powdered sugar
1 cup all-purpose flour
½ cup unsalted butter, diced and frozen for 20 minutes

*Topping:*
½ cup unsalted butter
¼ cup packed light brown sugar
¼ cup honey
2 tablespoons maple syrup
2 tablespoons heavy cream
12 soft caramels
8 ounces chopped pecans

Preheat oven to 325°. Line the bottom and sides of a 9" x 13" baking pan with parchment paper; set aside.

Place the sugar and flour in a food processor work bowl and process to blend. Add butter and pulse just to a coarse meal. Press mixture evenly into the pan. Bake the crust for 15 - 18 minutes, or until it is lightly golden.

While crust is baking, combine all topping ingredients, except pecans, in a saucepan. Cook over medium-high heat until mixture comes to a boil. Remove from heat, stir in pecans and pour over the hot crust.

Return to the oven and bake for an additional 20 minutes. Cool in the pan on a wire rack. When completely cool, lift parchment from pan and place on a cutting board; cut as desired.

# Lemon Bars

*Crust:*
1½ cups all-purpose flour
½ cup powdered sugar
¼ teaspoon kosher salt
¾ cup unsalted butter, diced and frozen for 20 minutes

*Topping:*
2¼ cups sugar
½ cup all-purpose flour
finely grated zest of 3 lemons
1 cup + 2 tablespoons fresh lemon juice (4 - 5 lemons)
6 large eggs, room temperature
1 egg yolk
pinch of kosher salt

powdered sugar

Preheat oven to 350°. Place flour, sugar and salt in a food processor work bowl and process to blend. Add butter and pulse just to a coarse meal. Press the dough evenly into the bottom of 9" x 13" baking pan. Bake the crust for about 30 minutes, or until it is a rich golden brown.

While crust is baking, whisk sugar and flour in a large bowl. Add lemon zest and juice, whisking to dissolve sugar.

In a separate bowl, whisk eggs, egg yolk and salt. Add eggs to lemon juice mixture and whisk vigorously to blend well.

When crust is browned, pull oven rack out and carefully pour topping onto the hot crust. Reduce oven temperature to 300° and bake for an additional 30 minutes, or until the filling is just firm.

Cool in the pan on a wire rack. When completely cool, sprinkle liberally with powdered sugar and cut as desired.

# Sherry Cake

1 box yellow cake mix
¾ cup canola oil
1 small box instant vanilla pudding
1 teaspoon ground nutmeg
½ cup dry sherry
4 large eggs, room temperature

powdered sugar

Preheat oven to 350°. Grease and flour a Bundt pan; set aside.

In the bowl of a stand mixer on medium-low speed, combine all ingredients in the order given, adding eggs one at a time. Scrape down sides as needed to blend thoroughly.

Pour batter evenly into the Bundt pan. Bake for 45 - 60 minutes, or until a tester comes out clean.

Cool in the pan on a wire rack for 15 minutes. Place a different wire rack over the pan and invert the cake onto the rack to finish cooling. When cool, transfer to a cake plate and dust lightly with powdered sugar.

# Double-Glazed Lemon Buttermilk Cake

*Just Desserts was widely known in San Francisco in the 1980's and 90's for their delectable sweets. The bakery's cakes and cookies were not the typical over-produced variety; they took homemade to a whole new level. This cake is adapted from a Just Desserts' recipe.*

*Cake:*
3 cups all-purpose flour
2 teaspoons baking powder
1 teaspoon salt
1 cup unsalted butter, room temperature
2 cups sugar
4 eggs, room temperature
1 cup buttermilk, room temperature
finely grated zest of 3 large lemons

*Glaze I:*
⅔ cup sugar
⅓ cup strained fresh lemon juice

*Glaze II:*
2 cups powdered sugar
3½ tablespoons strained fresh lemon juice

Preheat oven to 350°. Grease and flour a Bundt pan; set aside.

Combine flour, powder and salt; set aside.

In the bowl of a stand mixer, beat butter and sugar for several minutes on medium-high speed until light and fluffy. Reduce speed to medium and add eggs one at a time, scraping down sides and blending each well.

Reduce speed to low and add the dry ingredients alternately with the buttermilk: add ⅓ dry, ½ cup buttermilk, ⅓ dry, ½ cup buttermilk and ⅓ dry, blending each addition until just incorporated. Fold in the zest.

Pour batter evenly into the Bundt pan. Bake for 50 - 60 minutes, or until a tester comes out clean. Cool in the pan on a wire rack for 5 minutes.

While the cake is cooling in the pan, make the first glaze by combining the sugar and lemon juice in a small saucepan. Heat over medium-low heat until hot, but not boiling.

Place a different wire rack over the Bundt pan and invert the cake onto the rack. Place a sheet of aluminum foil under the rack and fold the edges up a bit. Using a pastry brush, apply the glaze immediately after it is heated, using all of it. Let the cake cool completely and transfer to a cake plate.

For the second glaze, whisk the powdered sugar and lemon juice until smooth. Drizzle over the cooled cake.

# Light Lemon Cake

*This cake would be lovely to serve with tea.*

*Cake:*
1¾ cups all-purpose flour
1 teaspoon baking soda
1 teaspoon baking powder
1 cup unsalted butter, room temperature
1 cup sugar
3 large eggs, room temperature
1 tablespoon finely grated lemon zest
2 teaspoons lemon extract
1 cup sour cream, room temperature

*Glaze:*
1½ cups powdered sugar
½ cup strained fresh lemon juice

Preheat oven to 350°. Grease and flour a Bundt pan; set aside.

Combine flour, soda and powder; set aside.

In the bowl of a stand mixer, beat butter and sugar on medium-high speed until light and fluffy. Reduce speed to medium and beat in eggs, lemon zest and extract, scraping down sides as needed to blend thoroughly; mix for 2 minutes.

On low speed, add half the flour mixture to the butter mixture; mix until well combined. Add half the sour cream; blend well. Add the remaining flour mixture, then the remaining sour cream. Mix until well combined.

Pour the batter evenly into the Bundt pan. Bake for 35 - 40 minutes, or until a tester comes out clean.

Cool in the pan on a wire rack for 10 minutes. While the cake cools, make the glaze by whisking the powdered sugar and lemon juice together until smooth.

Place a different wire rack over the pan and invert the cake onto the rack. Place a sheet of aluminum foil under the rack and fold the edges up a bit. Using a long skewer, poke holes into the cake almost to the bottom.

Apply the glaze while the cake is hot by slowly pouring the glaze over the cake, allowing it to absorb as you pour. When the cake has cooled to room temperature, transfer to a cake plate.

# Apple Cake

2 cups all-purpose flour
1 cup sugar
1 cup packed light brown sugar
1 teaspoon baking soda
1 teaspoon ground cinnamon
<1 teaspoon kosher salt
1 cup canola oil
3 large eggs, room temperature
1½ teaspoons pure vanilla extract
2 Granny Smith apples, peeled and chopped

Preheat oven to 350°. In a medium bowl, whisk dry ingredients. In a large bowl, whisk oil, eggs and vanilla until well blended. Blend dry ingredients into the egg mixture; batter will be very thick. Stir in apples.

Transfer the batter to a greased 9" x 13" baking pan. Bake for 30 - 35 minutes, or until a tester comes out clean.

Suggestion~
Add ½ cup chopped toasted walnuts.

# Carrot Cake

*This has been Julia's birthday cake since she was in preschool. I can't imagine her ever requesting any other!*

*Cake:*
smidge of butter
2 cups all-purpose flour
2 teaspoons baking soda
2 teaspoons ground cinnamon
1 teaspoon kosher salt
1½ cups unsalted butter, room temperature
2 cups sugar
4 large eggs, room temperature
1½ tablespoons pure vanilla extract
3 cups grated carrots

*Frosting:*
8 ounces cream cheese, room temperature
½ cup unsalted butter, room temperature
1 tablespoon pure vanilla extract
1-pound box powdered sugar

toasted walnut halves or chopped walnuts

Preheat oven to 350°. Butter and flour two 8" x 2" or 9" x 2" cake pans. Lay pans on a sheet of parchment and lightly draw the outline of the pan. Cut out the circles of parchment and butter one side. Place butter-side down in pans; set aside.

Combine flour, soda, cinnamon and salt; set aside.

In the bowl of a stand mixer, beat butter and sugar for several minutes on medium-high speed until light and fluffy.

Reduce speed to low and add the dry ingredients alternately with the eggs: Add ⅓ dry, 2 eggs, ⅓ dry, 2 eggs and ⅓ dry, blending each addition until just incorporated. Add vanilla and blend well. Fold in carrots.

Divide batter equally between the pans. Bake for about 40 minutes, or until a tester comes out clean.

Cool in the pans on a wire rack for 10 minutes. Run a table knife around the sides and place a different wire rack over each of the pans. Invert each cake onto the wire rack. Carefully peel off the parchment and allow the cakes to cool completely before frosting.

In an electric mixer with paddle attachment, beat cream cheese and butter on medium speed until well blended; add vanilla. Reduce speed to low and slowly add powdered sugar, beating constantly.

Place one of the layers, flat-side down, on a cake plate. Using 4 4"-wide strips of wax paper, slide one strip under the edge of cake. Repeat all around the cake so the plate is covered.

Frost the top of the layer evenly and place the second layer, flat-side up, on top of the frosted layer. Frost the top and sides of the cake. After the cake is frosted, remove wax strips one at a time by sliding one to the side as you pull it towards you.

Decorate the top perimeter or the bottom edge of the cake with walnuts.


Suggestion~
Add any of the following when folding the carrots into the cake:
shredded sweetened coconut
crushed pineapple, well drained
golden raisins
black currants
chopped toasted walnuts

# Faint-A-Lot
# aka Quadruple Chocolate Cake

*This is my mom's name for a deliciously chocolaty Bundt cake. She began making this when I was in college and I think of her every time I make it.*

*Cake:*
½ cup unsalted butter, room temperature
3 large eggs, room temperature
1 cup sour cream, room temperature
1 small box instant fudge pudding
1 box chocolate fudge or devil's food cake mix
¾ cup warm water
12-ounce package milk or semi-sweet chocolate chips

*Frosting:*
6 tablespoons unsalted butter
3 1-ounce squares semi-sweet chocolate
1½ teaspoons pure vanilla extract
2¼ cups powdered sugar
milk

~

Preheat oven to 350°. Grease and flour a Bundt pan; set aside.

In the bowl of a stand mixer, beat butter on medium-high speed until light and fluffy. Reduce speed to medium and add eggs, one at a time, scraping down sides as needed to blend thoroughly. Add sour cream and blend well.

Add the dry pudding to the dry cake mix (while it is in the bag) and stir to combine a bit. Reduce to low speed and the pudding/cake mix alternately with the water: Add ⅓ dry, ½ wet, ⅓ dry, ½ wet and ⅓ dry, blending each addition until incorporated. Stir in the chips.

Pour batter evenly into the Bundt pan. Bake for 50 - 60 minutes, or until cake springs back when lightly pressed and is just starting to pull away from the sides.

Place the pan on a wire rack and cool for 15 minutes. Invert onto a cake plate and cool completely before frosting.

In a 4-cup glass measure, microwave butter and chocolate on High for 1 minute. Whisk until fully melted and let cool. Whisk in vanilla and gradually whisk in powdered sugar, dribbling in a little milk if mixture is too thick. When all sugar is added, add enough milk until desired consistency is reached. Pour evenly over top of cake; allowing it drip down the sides.

# Poppy Seed Cake

1 box yellow cake mix
½ cup canola oil
1 small box instant vanilla pudding
⅔ cup dry sherry
1 cup sour cream, room temperature
⅓ cup poppy seeds
4 large eggs, room temperature

Preheat oven to 350°. Grease and flour a Bundt pan; set aside.

In the bowl of a stand mixer, combine all ingredients in the order given on medium-low speed, adding eggs one at a time and scraping down sides as needed to blend thoroughly.

Pour the batter evenly into the Bundt pan. Bake for about 45 - 60 minutes, or until a tester comes out clean.

Cool in the pan on a wire rack for 10 minutes. Place a different wire rack over the pan and invert the cake onto the rack to finish cooling.

# Flourless Chocolate Espresso Cake with Raspberry Sauce

*This cake is so rich and decadent, with the taste and texture reminiscent of a chocolate truffle.*

*Cake:*
16 ounces bittersweet chocolate, broken into small pieces
2 cups unsalted butter
½ cup freshly brewed espresso
½ cup water
1 cup packed light brown sugar
8 large eggs, room temperature and beaten

fresh raspberries
whipping cream, lightly sweetened and gently whipped

Preheat oven to 350°. Line the bottom of 9" x 2" round cake pan with parchment. Place it in a larger pan, such as a roasting pan; set aside.

Place chocolate in a large bowl. In a saucepan, bring butter, espresso, water and sugar to a boil, whisking to dissolve sugar. Pour over the chocolate and whisk until smooth. Let cool about 10 minutes, whisking occasionally. Add a few tablespoons of the chocolate mixture to the eggs, then whisk in eggs.

Pour batter evenly into the cake pan. Pour enough hot water into the larger pan to come halfway up the sides of the cake pan. Bake for about 1 hour, or until the center of cake is set and a tester comes out with just a few crumbs attached. Remove pan from water bath and cool completely on a wire rack. Cover with plastic wrap and refrigerate overnight.

Before serving, let cake sit at room temperature for about 25 minutes. Run a table knife around the sides of the pan to loosen the cake. Using oven mitts, hold the pan bottom over low heat for 15 seconds, to warm slightly. Place a cake plate over the pan and invert. Lift off cake pan and peel off parchment.

To serve, puddle some sauce on a plate, top with narrow wedge of cake and garnish with berries and freshly whipped cream.

Suggestion~
If you prefer not to brew the espresso, pick up ½ cup espresso from your local coffee house.

# Raspberry Sauce

2 12-ounce bags flash-frozen raspberries, thawed
¼ cup Grand Marnier, or to taste
2 teaspoons sugar, or to taste

Place half of the ingredients in a food processor work bowl. Blend until the raspberries are well blended and transfer to a bowl. Repeat with the remaining half.

Place a mesh strainer over a separate bowl and spoon some of the purée into the strainer. Press it with the back of a spoon until only seeds are left. Discard seeds and repeat until all purée is strained. Taste and adjust flavor. Cover and refrigerate.

# Molten Chocolate Cakes

*Not only are these warm, chocolate deliciousness, they may be made a day in advance and baked off right before serving. Since they are ideal for entertaining, I've included measurements for a dinner party of any size.*

| 2 | 4 | 6 | 8 |
|---|---|---|---|
| semi-sweet chocolate: | | | |
| 2⅓ oz | 4⅔ oz | 7 oz | 9⅓ oz |
| unsalted butter: | | | |
| 3 T + 1 t | 6 T + 2 t | 10 T | 13 T + 1 t |
| large egg/s, room temperature: | | | |
| 1 | 2 | 3 | 4 |
| egg yolk/s: | | | |
| 1 | 2 | 3 | 4 |
| pure vanilla extract: | | | |
| ⅓ t | ⅔ t | 1 t | 1⅓ t |
| powdered sugar: | | | |
| ½ c | 1 c | 1½ c | 2 c |
| all-purpose flour: | | | |
| 2 T + 2 t | 5 T + 1 t | ½ c | ½ c + 2 T + 2t |

powdered sugar
vanilla or coffee ice cream
fresh raspberries or sliced strawberries

Generously grease 2, 4, 6 or 8 6-ounce Pyrex custard cups; set aside.

Preheat oven to 450°. In a small saucepan, stir chocolate and butter over low heat until melted; cool slightly.

Whisk egg/s, egg yolk/s and vanilla in a bowl with a pour spout or a large glass measure. Whisk in sugar, then chocolate mixture and flour. Pour batter into custard cups, dividing equally.

Set cups on a rimmed baking sheet. Bake for about 11 minutes, or until the sides are set and center is soft and runny. Run a knife around the sides of the cups to loosen the cake. Cool 5 minutes; invert each onto a dessert plate.

Serve with a dusting of powdered sugar, small scoop of ice cream and berries.


Suggestion~
To make ahead and bake later, cover the cups with plastic wrap and refrigerate up to 36 hours. Increase the baking time to 14 minutes.

# Black Bottom Cupcakes

*Filling:*
8-ounce package cream cheese, room temperature
1 large egg
⅓ cup sugar
⅛ teaspoon kosher salt
1 cup mini chocolate chips

*Cake:*
1½ cups all-purpose flour
1 cup sugar
1 teaspoon baking soda
¼ cup unsweetened cocoa powder
½ teaspoon kosher salt
1 cup water
⅓ cup canola oil
1 tablespoon white vinegar
1 teaspoon pure vanilla extract

~

In the bowl of a stand mixer, beat all filling ingredients, except chips, on medium speed until smooth. Stir in chips; set aside.

in a large bowl, combine dry ingredients. Make a well and add remaining ingredients; stir until well blended.

Preheat oven to 350°. Spray two 24-cup mini-size or two 12-cup regular-size cupcake pans with cooking spray. For mini-size cupcake pans, place a scant 1 tablespoon cake batter in each cup. Top with a little more than ½ tablespoon of filling. For regular-size cupcake pans, place a scant ¼ cup cake batter in 18 cups. Top with a rounded 1 tablespoonful of filling.

Bake about 17 minutes for minis and about 25 minutes for regulars, or until the cake springs back when touched. Let cool on a wire rack 10 minutes. Run a knife around each cupcake and gently lift it out of the pan and place on a different wire rack to continue cooling.

Makes 48 mini-size or 18 regular-size cupcakes.

Suggestion~

If you prefer to bake this in a less labor-intensive way, pour about ⅔ of the cake batter into a greased and floured 9" x 13" baking pan. Spoon dollops of filling evenly over the batter and pour the remaining batter over the filling. Using the tip of a sharp knife, swirl the top layer of batter and filling together. Bake at 350° for about 30 minutes, or until the cake springs back when touched or a tester comes out clean.

# White Chocolate Cheesecake
# with Dark Chocolate Leaves

*Garnishing the cheesecake with chocolate leaves creates a beautiful presentation.*

*Cheesecake:*
30 chocolate wafer cookies
6 - 8 tablespoons melted unsalted butter
2 pounds cream cheese, room temperature
½ cup unsalted butter, room temperature
4 large eggs, room temperature
12 ounces white chocolate, melted and cooled
1 tablespoon + 2 teaspoons pure vanilla extract
¼ teaspoon kosher salt

*Leaves:*
3 - 4 ounces semi-sweet chocolate, melted
8 - 10 camellia or lemon leaves, with stems attached

Break up cookies in a food processor work bowl and process until there are fine crumbs. Add melted butter and process until combined. Press into the bottom and sides of a 9" springform pan. Refrigerate several hours.

Preheat oven to 300°. In the bowl of a stand mixer, beat cheese and butter on medium-high speed until smooth. Add eggs one at a time, blending well after each addition and scraping sides as needed. Add chocolate, vanilla and salt; beat 1 - 2 minutes at medium speed.

Pour mixture into the springform and bake for 1 hour. Cool in the pan on a wire rack for 2 hours. Cover with plastic wrap and refrigerate. Refrigerate overnight before serving.

For the leaves, dip the backside of a spoon in chocolate and coat the underside of each leaf with chocolate, bringing the chocolate almost to the edge of the leaf. Place on a plate and refrigerate until hardened.

Take one leaf from the refrigerator and separate the chocolate from the leaf by carefully peeling the leaf from the stem end; place the chocolate leaf back on the plate. Repeat with remaining leaves. Arrange the leaves decoratively around the perimeter of the cheesecake.

# Mini Pecan Tarts

*Dough:*
3 ounces cream cheese
½ cup unsalted butter
1 cup all-purpose flour
⅛ teaspoon kosher salt

*Filling:*
1 egg
1 tablespoon unsalted butter, melted
¾ cup packed light brown sugar
1 teaspoon pure vanilla extract
1 cup chopped pecans

Place cream cheese and butter in a food processor work bowl and process to blend. Add flour and salt; process/pulse until dough forms a ball. Divide dough evenly in half.

In a bowl, beat the egg and add remaining filling ingredients, except pecans, blending well.

Preheat oven to 350°. Using one of the dough halves, press a small amount of dough into the bottom and up the sides of a cup in a 24-cup mini-size cupcake pan. Continue working the dough to create shells in all the cups. Add about a ½ tablespoon of the filling to each shell. Add a little more than 1 teaspoon of pecans to each. Repeat with remaining dough and a second pan.

Bake for about 20 minutes, or until shells brown and filling gets dark. Let cool on a wire rack about 8 minutes. Gently slide a knife down the side of the tarts and lift the tarts out. Place the tarts on a different wire rack to cool completely.

# Pecan Fudge Tart

*Crust:*
1½ cups all-purpose flour
¼ cup sugar
pinch kosher salt
1½ cups unsalted butter, diced and frozen for 20 minutes
1 egg yolk
3 tablespoons heavy or whipping cream

*Filling:*
3 ounces semi-sweet chocolate
2 ounces unsweetened chocolate
¼ cup unsalted butter
4 large eggs, room temperature
1 cup sugar
1 cup dark corn syrup
½ teaspoon kosher salt
2 teaspoons pure vanilla extract
2 cups pecan halves

Place flour, sugar and salt in a food processor work bowl and process to blend. Add butter and process/pulse until mixture resembles coarse meal. Beat yolk and cream in a small bowl. With processor running, add yolk mixture through the feed tube and mix until dough just comes together. Gather dough into a ball and flatten into a disk. Roll out on a floured surface to ¼" thick. Place in an 11" tart pan with removable bottom, pressing dough into the rim; trim edges. Freeze 15 minutes.

Preheat oven to 400°. Cover pastry with aluminum foil and fill with dry beans or pie weights. Bake 15 minutes. Carefully lift foil and beans/weights out of the pan; bake an additional 5 minutes. Cool on a wire rack. Keep oven set at 400°.

In a large microwaveable bowl, melt chocolates and butter in microwave until almost melted. Stir and let cool a bit.

In a separate bowl, whisk eggs, sugar, corn syrup and salt. Slowly whisk the egg mixture into the warm chocolate mixture. Add vanilla, then pecans.

Pour into the crust and bake for 5 minutes; reduce oven temperature to 350°. Bake an additional 30 minutes, or until tart puffs in center and is just set. Cool on a wire rack.

# Pumpkin Pie

*Crust:*
1¼ cups all-purpose flour
½ cup powdered sugar
½ cup unsalted butter, diced and frozen for 20 minutes
3 tablespoons heavy or whipping cream

*Filling:*
3 large eggs, room temperature
16-ounce can pumpkin
¾ cup heavy or whipping cream, room temperature
½ cup sour cream, room temperature
¾ cup sugar
1 tablespoon brown sugar
1 tablespoon cornstarch
¾ teaspoon powdered ginger
¼ teaspoon kosher salt
¼ cup apricot jam

~

Combine flour and sugar in a food processor work bowl; add butter and pulse/process to blend. With machine running, add cream and process until moist clumps form. Gather dough into a ball and flatten into a disk. Wrap in plastic wrap and refrigerate 15 minutes.

Preheat oven to 350°. Roll out dough on a lightly floured surface; transfer to pie plate. Trim overhang to 1" and fold under; pinch around edges. Cover pastry with aluminum foil and fill with dry beans or pie weights. Bake for 10 minutes. Carefully lift foil and beans/weights out of pan; bake an additional 10 minutes. Reduce oven temperature to 325°.

Make the filling when the crust has about 10 minutes to finish baking. Beat the eggs in a medium bowl. Stir in pumpkin, cream and sour cream. Add the dry ingredients, blending well.

Spread jam over the hot crust; pour in filling. Bake until almost set, about 55 minutes. Cool completely on a wire rack, wrap well in plastic wrap and refrigerate.

Best made one day before serving.

# French Apple Tart with Caramel Sauce

*I love caramel apples in the fall so much that I became inspired to create this beautiful tart.*

*Tart dough:*
2 cups all-purpose flour
½ teaspoon kosher salt
1 tablespoon sugar
12 tablespoons unsalted butter, diced and frozen for 20 minutes
½ cup ice water

*Apples:*
4 Granny Smith apples
2 tablespoons sugar
>¼ teaspoon ground cinnamon (if not serving with Caramel Sauce, use ½
   teaspoon, or more, to taste)
2 tablespoons unsalted butter, melted

Combine flour, salt and sugar in a food processor work bowl; pulse a few times to blend. Add butter and pulse about 10 times or until butter is pea-sized. With machine running, pour ice water through feed tube and pulse until dough just begins to come together. Sprinkle some flour on a board and gather dough to form a ball, then flatten the ball into a rectangle. Wrap in plastic wrap and refrigerate 2 hours.

On a floured board, roll the dough into a 10" x 14" rectangle. Trim the sides so all are straight. Place the dough on a large rimmed baking sheet lined with parchment. Refrigerate dough while prepping the apples.

Preheat oven to 400°. Peel apples and cut each in half through the stem. Remove stems using a knife and remove cores using a melon baller. Slice apples ¼" crosswise and discard ends. Remove pan from refrigerator and with the long side of the pan facing you, fan two halves vertically as you lay them on the pastry to create a column of overlapping apples, all curving down, so that the two halves complete the left column. (Leave a ¼" border on the edge and at the top and bottom.) Repeat overlapping slices of 2 more halves next to the first column, but have them curving up. Repeat with remaining apples, alternating the direction of the apples and creating a total of 4 columns.

Combine sugar and cinnamon. Brush the apples with melted butter and sprinkle cinnamon sugar evenly over all.

Bake 45 - 60 minutes, until the tart is browned. Serve warm or at room temperature, with or without a Caramel Sauce drizzle.


# Caramel Sauce

*Caramel sauce is quick to make, about 15 minutes, but getting it just the right shade of 'caramel' can be tricky. Be patient... it may take more than one attempt, but it's so worth it!*

1 cup sugar
6 tablespoons unsalted butter, cubed and room temperature
½ cup heavy cream, room temperature
>½ teaspoon flaky sea salt

~

In a heavy 3-quart saucepan, melt sugar over medium heat, using a silicone spatula to gently stir as sugar melts. As soon as sugar melts, stop stirring. Color will change from golden to a golden-brown with red streaks. Swirl the pan gently so colors blend. Cook until it becomes a deep amber color; the darker the color, the less sweet and richer the caramel will be. Take care, however, as allowing the color to get too dark can result in burnt sugar.

As soon as it reaches the desired color, remove from heat and, using a whisk, add butter, whisking quickly until melted. Slowly pour in the cream, whisking until caramel is smooth. Whisk in salt.

Let cool a few minutes and pour into a mason jar. Cool completely before covering and storing in the refrigerator.

*For the tart:* It is important to pour the caramel sauce immediately before serving, to avoid the tart becoming soggy. To drizzle caramel sauce onto the tart slices, have the tart and the sauce at room temperature. Place the slices of tart on individual dessert plates. Transfer about ½ cup of sauce to a small zip-top bag and cut a very tiny corner of the bag. Squeeze the bag gently as the sauce is drizzled diagonally over the apples.


Caramel sauce can be stored in the refrigerator up to 2 weeks. Reheat in a small microwaveable bowl on Medium power in 20-second increments until sauce is just pourable.

# Rustic Apple Pie

*The 'rusticness' of this pie is due to look of the crust. It doesn't have a top crust; the bottom crust is rolled out larger than usual and folds up and over most of the apples, giving it an uneven and rustic appearance.*

*Crust:*
1 cup all-purpose flour
1 teaspoon sugar
½ teaspoon kosher salt
½ cup unsalted butter, diced and frozen for 20 minutes
2 tablespoons ice water

*Filling:*
5 Granny Smith apples, peeled and thinly sliced
½ cup sugar
1 teaspoon ground cinnamon
⅛ teaspoon ground nutmeg

2 tablespoons unsalted butter, diced

Place flour, sugar and salt in a food processor work bowl and process to blend. Toss in butter and process/pulse just until mixture is crumbly. With machine running, add ice water a little at a time through the feed tube, until dough pulls away from the bowl and forms a solid mass.

Remove dough and knead once or twice on a lightly floured surface. Flatten into a disk and wrap in plastic wrap; refrigerate 20 minutes.

Preheat oven to 375°. While the dough chills, make the filling by combining all ingredients together in a large bowl.

On a floured surface, roll the dough into a 12" circle and place in an 8" pie plate. Fill with apples, arranging apples evenly; dot with butter. Fold pastry edges up and over the apples; there will be an opening in the center.

Bake for 45 - 50 minutes, or until filling is bubbly and crust is golden.

# Blueberry Pie

*The beauty of this filling is that it retains a fresh berry taste and texture since the majority of berries do not get cooked. To quote Julia, "It is the ultimate summer dessert!"*

½ cup sugar
¼ teaspoon kosher salt
1 tablespoon + 2 teaspoons cornstarch
⅔ cup water
4 heaping cups fresh blueberries, divided
1½ tablespoons unsalted butter
1½ tablespoons fresh lemon juice
1 baked and cooled pie shell

Combine dry ingredients in a saucepan. Add water, mixing well and cook over medium heat, stirring constantly. When the mixture is hot, add ½ cup blueberries and continue stirring. If the mixture begins to boil as it thickens, reduce the heat a bit, and continue to cook until it has a glaze-like consistency. Remove from heat and stir in butter. When butter is melted, stir in juice.

Let the mixture cool about 10 minutes until lukewarm, stirring occasionally. Gently stir in remaining berries and pour the filling into the pie shell. Refrigerate at least 8 hours or overnight before serving.

# Baklava

*When the girls were young, I would make this every year around Christmas. It was quite a production, but well worth it. The baklava was one of those wonderful homemade gifts to give... and, of course, it was pretty wonderful having it in the house.*

*Syrup:*
2 cups water
4 cups sugar
<¼ cup honey
2 cinnamon sticks
zest of 1 orange
1 teaspoon pure vanilla extract

*Filling:*
2 pounds toasted walnuts, chopped medium to fine
⅔ cup sugar
2 teaspoons ground cinnamon

2½ cups unsalted butter, melted + more, if needed
1 pound frozen phyllo, refrigerated overnight to thaw

Combine syrup ingredients in a saucepan and bring to a boil, stirring continuously. Reduce heat, continue stirring and simmer for 10 minutes. Remove from heat and let stand for 30 minutes. Discard cinnamon sticks and strain into a 4-cup glass measure or a bowl; set aside to cool.

For filling, combine walnuts, sugar and cinnamon in a large bowl, stirring to thoroughly coat nuts; set aside.

Use a new 2"-wide paintbrush (see Details, page 9) and brush a 12½" x 17½" rimmed baking sheet with melted butter. Place a sheet of phyllo over butter. Brush generously with butter, layer another phyllo sheet, brush with butter, and continue layering and brushing until you've used 8 sheets.

Spread 2 cups of the nut mixture evenly over the phyllo. Cover with a sheet of phyllo, brush with butter and repeat until you've used 3 sheets of phyllo. Follow layering instructions on the next page, brushing each sheet of phyllo with butter.

Layering from *bottom to top:*
- 8 sheets
- 2 cups nuts
- 3 sheets
- 2 cups nuts
- 3 sheets
- 2 cups nuts
- 3 sheets
- 2 cups nuts
- 8 - 10 sheets – on this last layering, butter both sides of the first sheet to go over the nuts; butter the top sheets very generously. Pour any remaining butter over the top sheet.

Preheat oven to 350°. Using a very sharp knife, cut the baklava into diamond- or square-shaped pieces. Bake for 30 minutes or until golden brown. Place the baking sheet on a wire rack and pour the cooled syrup evenly over all, penetrating the layers and covering the baklava. Cool completely and cover tightly with plastic wrap. Let rest overnight.

Do not refrigerate. Serve pieces in paper-lined foil mini-size cupcake cups. If kept tightly wrapped, baklava will stay fresh for up to 2 weeks.


Suggestion~
To cut the same size diamond-shape pieces, wrap a yardstick in plastic. With long side of the pan facing you, set the yardstick on a diagonal over the phyllo in the lower left corner; cut on right side of stick. Move the yardstick so the cut is on the left side and again cut on the right side of the stick. Continue moving the yardstick and cutting until done. Turn the pan so the short side is facing you. Place the yardstick in the lower left corner on a diagonal and continue cutting and moving the yardstick across the pan. When finished, the baklava will be cut into diamond shapes. This will yield little triangle-shaped pieces along the sides of the pan... perfect to nibble on!

# Apple Crisp

*Our family has been enjoying this for as long as I can remember. Although it's typically served warm, it also tastes delicious cold, right out of the refrigerator.*

*Topping:*
¾ cup all-purpose flour
¼ cup sugar
½ cup packed light brown sugar
1½ teaspoons ground cinnamon
½ teaspoon kosher salt
6 tablespoons unsalted butter, diced and frozen for 20 minutes

*Filling:*
6 Granny Smith apples, peeled and thickly sliced
½ lemon, juiced
¼ cup sugar
2 tablespoons all-purpose flour

vanilla ice cream, if desired

Preheat oven to 375°. Place dry ingredients in a food processor work bowl and process to blend. Toss in butter and pulse until it is the consistency of coarse meal. Set the topping aside.

Place the apples in 9" x 13" baking pan and toss with lemon juice. Toss again with sugar and flour. Arrange the apples evenly in the pan and sprinkle the topping evenly over the apples.

Bake for 35 - 40 minutes until bubbly and lightly browned. Let cool for 15 minutes. Serve warm with ice cream.


Suggestion~
The topping can be made ahead and kept refrigerated for several days or can be kept frozen in a freezer zip-top bag until ready to use.

An apple corer/slicer that cuts an apple into 8 wedges works well to give uniformed slices that cook evenly.

# Tiramisu

1 cup finely ground espresso
1½ cups water
6 large egg yolks, room temperature
⅔ cup sugar, divided
3 cups mascarpone
¼ cup sweet Marsala
4 large egg whites, room temperature
3 3-ounce packages soft ladyfingers
unsweetened cocoa powder

~

In a coffee maker, brew espresso with the water. Pour into a bowl and set aside to cool completely.

Trim one end of the ladyfingers so they are the same height as a 9" springform pan when vertical. Quickly dip flat side of ladyfingers in the espresso and stand them up, flat side facing in and cut side down, around the perimeter of the pan. Cover bottom of pan with the quickly-dipped ladyfingers. (Trim the ladyfingers accordingly to fit in the pan.)

In the bowl of a stand mixer, beat egg yolks with all but 2 tablespoons sugar for about 5 minutes, or until thick and pale yellow. Add mascarpone and Marsala, scraping down sides and blending until well combined; set aside.

Using whip attachment, beat whites with the remaining 2 tablespoons sugar until firm, but not stiff, peaks form. Fold whites into mascarpone mixture.

Cover ladyfingers in pan with ⅓ of mascarpone mixture and dust with cocoa. Repeat layering with additional ladyfingers (not dipped) and mascarpone two more times.

Cover pan tightly with plastic wrap and refrigerate overnight.


Suggestion~
If you prefer not to brew the espresso, pick up 1½ cups espresso from your local coffee house.

# Custard
## aka French Cream

*When I was growing up, my mom would make individual fruit and cream tarts for dinner parties. They were just beautiful and the custard filling was divine!*

½ cup sugar
¼ cup all-purpose flour
2 tablespoons cornstarch
⅛ teaspoon kosher salt
¼ cup cold milk + more, if desired
2 large egg yolks
2 cups warm milk
1 tablespoon unsalted butter
1 teaspoon pure vanilla extract

fresh berries

~

In a 2-quart saucepan, whisk dry ingredients.

In a 1-cup glass measure, whisk cold milk with egg yolks. Pour the mixture gradually into the saucepan, whisking until smooth.

Slowly add warm milk, whisking until well blended. Cook over medium heat until thick, whisking continuously. When mixture begins to bubble, reduce to medium-low and simmer 5 minutes. Remove from heat and whisk in butter.

Whisk custard occasionally while it cools. When cool, add vanilla and refrigerate at least 8 hours. Stir custard, and if it is too thick, thin with some milk to desired consistency.

Serving in bowls with berries.


Suggestion~
Place the filling in individual tart shells and top with fresh berries.

# Grand Marnier Freeze

1 tablespoon light brown sugar
¼ cup Grand Marnier
5 cups softened vanilla ice cream

In a small bowl, stir sugar and liqueur until sugar dissolves. Place the ice cream in a food processor work bowl and pulse several times. Add liqueur and blend thoroughly. Taste and add additional liqueur, if desired.

Pour into martini glasses or small bowls, cover with plastic wrap and place in the freezer for at least 6 hours before serving or pour into drinking glasses and serve as adult milkshakes.


Suggestion~
The Grand Marnier may be substituted with other liqueurs, such as Amaretto or Kahlua.

Pre-freezing the martini glasses or bowls will help the softened ice cream harden faster.

# Chocolate Crunch Ice Cream Cake

*Laura has a summer birthday, making this her perfect birthday cake. Her favorite two ice cream flavors for this are peppermint and vanilla. This is terrific with any two ice cream flavors that go well with each other and go well with chocolate... and what doesn't go well with chocolate?*

*Crunch:*
¾ cup semi-sweet chocolate chips
<1 tablespoon canola oil
9-ounce package chocolate wafer cookies

*Crust:*
9-ounce package chocolate wafer cookies
7 tablespoons unsalted butter, melted
2 1-quart ice creams, softened

Place chips and oil in a microwaveable bowl and heat until almost melted. Stir until melted and let cool; set aside.

Break one package of cookies into a food processor work bowl and process until crumbly. Pour the melted chocolate over the cookie crumbs; pulse to blend. Spread chocolate crumbs on an aluminum foil-lined rimmed baking sheet; freeze to harden. Do not wash work bowl.

Preheat oven to 325°. Break second package of cookies into the food processor work bowl and process until crumbly. With the machine running, add butter through the feed tube and process until well mixed.

Butter a 9" or 9½" springform pan and press crumb mixture into the bottom and sides. Bake for 10 minutes; cool on a wire rack.

When completely cool, scoop 1 quart of ice cream into the pan. Place a sheet of plastic wrap directly on the ice cream and use your hands to press and create a smooth top; discard plastic wrap. Sprinkle half the crunch over it and press in lightly. Freeze for 20 minutes.

Spread remaining quart of ice cream on top of crunch and repeat the pressing using plastic wrap. Sprinkle remaining crunch over and press in lightly. Wrap pan tightly in plastic wrap, then aluminum foil. Freeze overnight.

Let stand at room temperature for 10 minutes before serving.


Suggestion~
For extra decadence, serve with Fudge Sauce (page 246).


# Chocolate Chip Cookie or Fudgy Brownie Ice Cream Sundae

Chocolate Chip Cookies (page 194), baking 1 cookie for each sundae
*or*
1 recipe Fudgy Brownies (page 208), cooled completely

ice cream, flavor of choice
Caramel Sauce (page 235)
Fudge Sauce (page 246)
Drunken Cherries (page 247)

*Chocolate Chip Cookie Ice Cream Sundae:*
Bake cookies and take them out of the oven a little under done. Let them cool for about 1 minute and place each in a bowl. Top with a scoop of ice cream and several spoonfuls of Fudge Sauce; serve immediately.

*Fudgy Brownie Ice Cream Sundae:*
Cut brownies to desired size and place each on a plate. Top with a scoop of ice cream and spoonfuls of Caramel Sauce, Fudge Sauce or Drunken Cherries; serve immediately.

# Fudge Sauce

*This is so delicious – not overly sweet and with great texture. It's not unusual to find someone (myself included!) eating it cold right out of the container!*

4 tablespoons unsalted butter
4 ounces unsweetened chocolate
¼ cup light corn syrup
1½ cups sugar
12-ounce can evaporated milk
1½ teaspoons pure vanilla extract

In a 2-quart saucepan, melt butter and unsweetened chocolate over medium heat. Stir in corn syrup and sugar. Slowly stir in milk.

Cook, stirring constantly for about 15 - 20 minutes, until sugar is completely dissolved and sauce thickens, reducing heat as needed so that sauce does not boil. Remove from heat and stir in vanilla. Serve slightly warm, not hot. Allow it to cool completely before refrigerating.

The sauce will keep in the refrigerator for several weeks... but probably won't!

Suggestion~
To reheat a small amount, place the desired amount in a small microwavable bowl and heat on Medium power until sauce is softened and warm. For larger amounts, reheat in a saucepan over medium-low heat, stirring until warmed through.

If you prefer a more complex chocolate taste, add 1½ - 2 ounces dark chocolate (about 70% cocoa).

# Drunken Cherries

*I love Ben & Jerry's Cherry Garcia. This cherry and wine sauce, paired with ice cream and shaved chocolate, is an adult interpretation of my favorite… and we all know how well red wine and dark chocolate go together!*

1½ cups zinfandel or pinot noir
¾ cup sugar
3 whole cloves
1½ pounds fresh dark cherries, pitted and halved
¼ teaspoon pure vanilla extract

vanilla ice cream
semi-sweet chocolate bar, shaved

In a saucepan, bring wine, sugar and cloves to a boil over medium heat, stirring until sugar dissolves. Reduce heat to keep an active simmer. Cook until wine mixture reduces to 1 cup; discard cloves.

Add cherries to the reduced wine mixture. Simmer for exactly 5 minutes, stirring occasionally and gently pressing the cherries into the liquid. Remove from heat and add vanilla. Let cool to room temperature, stirring occasionally. Store in the refrigerator.

Serve chilled over ice cream and topped with chocolate shavings.


Suggestion~
Create chocolate shavings by running a vegetable peeler down the side of the chocolate bar; results are best when the bar is slightly warm.

# Peanut Butter Squares

*I've been making these for many, many years. They freeze well, so I bring them to family when visiting. Actually, I'm not sure they'd let me in the door without them! When they come to visit me and see the signature white tin in the refrigerator, they always know what's in it.*

1 cup unsalted butter
2¼ cups powdered sugar
1 cup crunchy peanut butter
1½ cups graham cracker crumbs
12-ounce package milk chocolate chips

In a large microwaveable bowl, melt butter on Medium power for 2 minutes, adding 20-second increments until butter is melted. Stir in sugar, peanut butter and crumbs separately, in the order given, until each is thoroughly blended. Pat the mixture evenly into a 9" x 13" baking pan.

Place chips in a microwaveable bowl and heat on High for 1 minute; stir. Heat in 20-second increments until chocolate is almost melted; stir until completely melted. Spread chocolate evenly over peanut butter mixture. Refrigerate for 30 minutes.

Remove from refrigerator and cut into squares. Refrigerate for another 30 minutes; re-cut. Store squares in a tin (not a plastic container), separating layers with wax paper. Keep refrigerated.

# English Toffee

1 cup salted butter
1 cup sugar
⅓ cup packed light brown sugar
2 tablespoons water
2 teaspoons pure vanilla extract
8-ounce bar good-quality semi-sweet chocolate, broken into 1" pieces
¾ cup toasted walnuts, finely chopped

Line a large rimmed baking sheet with parchment paper; set aside.

Clip a candy thermometer to the inside of a heavy 2- or 3-quart saucepan. Cut each stick of butter into 5 or 6 pieces and place in the saucepan along with the sugars and water. Bring to a boil over medium heat, stirring gently and constantly with a heat-resistant silicone spatula. Continue to gently stir, taking care to scrap the bottom and sides of the saucepan, until the temperature reaches 300°. Remove from heat and stir in vanilla, blending well.

Pour it immediately onto the parchment paper and quickly spread it to a thin layer. (An offset spatula works well.) Let toffee cool for about 10 minutes.

Melt chocolate in a microwaveable bowl on High for 45 seconds. Stir it continuously for 2 -3 minutes, or until it is completely melted. Gently wipe toffee with paper towels, then spread chocolate evenly to cover. Sprinkle walnuts evenly over the chocolate. Place a sheet of wax paper over the nuts and gently pat them into the chocolate. Let stand at room temperature until chocolate is set and has a matte finish.

Refrigerate toffee until chocolate is hard, and then carefully break it into pieces. Store in a tin (not a plastic container), separating each layer with wax paper. Keep refrigerated; serve at room temperature.


Suggestion~
Do not make toffee if the weather is humid.

If you're partial to a salty-sweet taste, sprinkle some flaky sea salt over the chocolate before sprinkling with the chopped walnuts.

# Millie's Bones

*Julia and Dave's sweet pup, Millie, loves these treats!*

2 large eggs
2 tablespoons canola oil
1 tablespoon honey
1 cup chicken broth
2 cups, less 2 tablespoons, whole-wheat flour
1¼ cups all-purpose flour
½ cup corn meal
1 cup smooth peanut butter

In a 2-cup glass measure, whisk eggs, oil and honey. Whisk in broth.

In the bowl of a stand mixer, combine dry ingredients on low speed. On medium-low speed, slowly pour in chicken broth mixture. Add peanut butter. Mix until dough comes together, about one minute.

Move oven racks to center of oven and preheat to 350°. Cover two cookie sheets with parchment; set aside.

Divide dough in half. Roll out to ⅛" on a lightly floured surface. Using a bone-shaped cookie cutter, cut out bones; re-roll scraps and cut out more bones. Place bones very close together on the cookie sheet. Repeat with remaining dough. Bake both sheets for 15 minutes. Rotate sheets and switch racks. Bake for an additional 15 minutes. Transfer to wire racks to cool.

# a ~ z

Warm Orzo Salad with Grilled Shrimp or Chicken • 60
Warm Spinach Salad with Poppy Seed Dressing • 59
Watermelon Feta Salad • 152
White Chocolate Cheesecake with Dark Chocolate Leaves • 230
White Chocolate Chip Chocolate Cookies • 195
White Corn Tortilla Soup • 47
Wild Mushroom Soup • 36
Zucchini Ribbons • 149

~

# Thank you...

for spending time with my family's favorites. Wishing you, and those gathered around your table, platefuls of happy eating as you all dig in!

Judy